Creative
BEADED
JEWELRY

33 Exquisite Designs Inspired by the Arts
of China, Japan, India and Tibet

By Carolyn Schulz

TUTTLE Publishing

Tokyo | Rutland, Vermont | Singapore

Contents

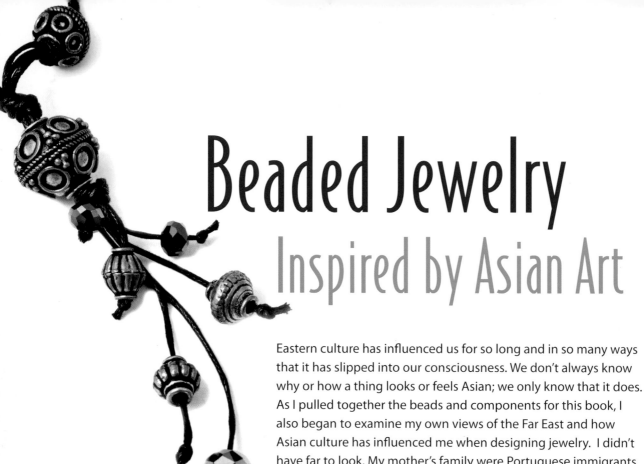

Beaded Jewelry
Inspired by Asian Art

Eastern culture has influenced us for so long and in so many ways that it has slipped into our consciousness. We don't always know why or how a thing looks or feels Asian; we only know that it does. As I pulled together the beads and components for this book, I also began to examine my own views of the Far East and how Asian culture has influenced me when designing jewelry. I didn't have far to look. My mother's family were Portuguese immigrants to the Hawaiian Islands, where East meets West. Cultural diversity abounds in every aspect of life from food to fabrics to religion to architecture, so it wasn't hard to see how Asian color and texture have become part of the creativity I so enjoy.

The arts of Asia can be highly practical or purely decorative. They range from the most austere and simple to the most ornate and intricate. The Eastern ability to observe, appreciate and capture beauty, especially the beauty of nature, is such that the most mundane objects can seem an act of worship.

Beads, too, have been a part of many cultures from time immemorial. They have served as currency, as well as ornaments, and even expressions of status. They have been invested with power and spiritual meaning and are a wonderful medium for creative expression.

This book aims to bring these two fascinating phenomena together. The designs included here borrow from the Asian use of color and texture as well as from aspects of Asian design. Some are simple pieces that can be completed in minutes, while others are more challenging but equally fun and rewarding. Hopefully, the designs in this book will inspire you to try variations and experiment with your own sense of Asian style.

NOTES ON MATERIALS AND TOOLS

Beads

Beads come in all shapes and sizes and in wide variety of materials, both natural and man made. They are available in every color, shade and hue you can imagine. Finding just the right color and texture can be the difference between a nice piece and a fabulous piece. Some people seem to have been born with the natural instinct for what goes best with what. I am not one of those people—it's through observation and experimentation that I have found my style and area of comfort. My advice, even to those with a great innate sense of style, is get out and about. Look at what people are wearing around you. Look at the colors and textures of beads in the pre-made jewelry being sold in the stores. Then, experiment by mixing and matching and finding exactly what works for your design.

Findings

For those of you completely new to beading, findings are the metal components used to hold the piece together. Clasps/closures, ear wires and jump rings all fall into this category. The right findings depend on the

weight of the piece and level of wear the piece will be exposed to, so be careful to choose accordingly. This book shows you just some of the many different styles that are out there so, again, get out and look around. You'll find that it's not unusual to build a piece around the perfect closure or ear wire—that's how beautiful some findings can be.

Cords, Threads and Wire

Cords, threads and wire come in a variety of different materials and strengths. While you'll see many different types in this book, new stringing materials are becoming available seemingly day by day. I encourage you to experiment with whatever appeals to your senses to create own unique jewelry.

You'll note that stringing material lengths are given in both inches and metrics. If your ruler doesn't offer metric measurements, it's a good idea to invest in one that does. Metric measurements are a bit more precise, which will be especially helpful when working with multiple strands of different lengths. The slight difference it makes in the drape of a piece can result in a more polished look.

Stringing

Cotton, leather, wire, ribbon, tubing—the list of wonderful stringing materials goes on and on. Pictured are some types used in the projects in this book (from top): Stringing wire comes in many strengths, thicknesses and colors. Cotton cord is also available in many colors and thicknesses, and can be waxed or not (waxed cord is more resistant to fraying). Memory wire comes in several gauges as well as in different coil sizes. The length you see here is suitable for bracelets. Larger coils are available for necklaces, smaller ones for rings. Elastic/stretch cord comes in different thickness, and in black as well as in clear.

Chains

Base metal chain is available in most craft stores. Precious metal chains, such as gold, gold-filled, sterling silver, and others can generally be found in bead shops or through online vendors.

Pins and Rings

Like most findings, head pins, eye pins and jump rings come in many sizes, thicknesses and materials, and are extremely versatile. A good assortment of these is invaluable. Most craft stores carry a basic variety. A wider selection of sizes, and materials can be purchased from bead vendors.

Crimps and Covers

Crimp tubes and beads vary in size and thickness to suit the many different types of stringing materials available. If a crimp detracts from the look of your piece, a matching crimp cover is a great fix.

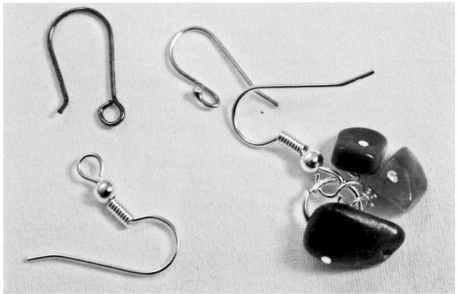

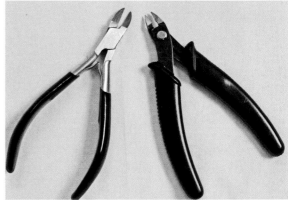

Clasps

(From top) Toggle clasps,
claw clasps and safety clasps are just
a few of the closures available. Some
clasps are beautiful enough to be
works of art in themselves.

Earring Findings

Earring findings come in a number of
forms, including hoops, posts,
threads and hooks. Pictured here are
different hook styles. Like clasps,
some earring findings are interesting
enough to be part of the design.

Tools

Many crafting tools are simply a
special version of everyday tools,
refined to fit the needs of the
crafting materials. Different cutters
are chosen according to the
material being cut and even the
angle at which the cut is being
made. Pliers can be round nosed for
wrapping, flat nosed for grasping
materials, and other shapes that
make metalworking easier.
Specialized tools such as a crimping
tool (more in chapter 3) and
memory wire shears (more in
chapter 2) are just a few of the
other tools jewelry crafters come to
invest in. And there's always

something new. Check major
beading sites on the internet for a
tour of tools and components. Many
sites offer full glossaries of beading/
jewelry making terms. If you're new
to the craft the internet is great
place to start.

CHAPTER 1
Elastic Cord Bracelets

Using Elastic Cord

Some may think that using elastic cord to make jewelry pieces is too simplistic, but with beautiful beads, quality components, a few technical tricks, and inspiration, anyone can achieve spectacular results, and all with minimal effort and time!

Basic technique for using elastic cord

Tie a **slipknot** at one end of elastic cord to keep beads from falling off before you're ready to tie off.
Thread your beads in the desired order.
Tie ends together in a **surgeon's knot**.
If the hole in a bead on either side of the knot is large enough, thread one tail of surgeon's knot back through that bead and pull gently until knot pops into bead.

Hints & tips

- Elastic cord comes in several different thicknesses Generally, the thicker it is, the stronger it is. Choose the one that works best for the beads you're using and for the sort of wear the bracelet will be exposed to.
- If you find that the cord is a tight fit with the bead holes, try cutting the end of cord at an angle.
- If the cord is the right thickness but won't pass through the bead, try using a bead reamer to clear away any blockages inside the bead (but be careful not to break it).
- When pulling to tighten the knot, don't just pull on the two tails of cord. Pull also on the inner strands.
- Use clear nail polish/varnish to seal and secure the knot.

Tying a slipknot

1 Form a loop.

2 Reach through the loop and take the short end by the middle, pulling it through in a loop.

3 Gently tug the loop until the knot tightens. You don't need this knot to be too tight. To undo, gently pull the tail.

Tying a surgeon's knot

This is the best knot when tying off stretchy cord.

1 Cross left end of cord over right end of cord, bring around once, then twice and pull.

2 Cross right end of cord over left end of cord and pull tight until knot catches.

3 Glue knot to seal and secure.

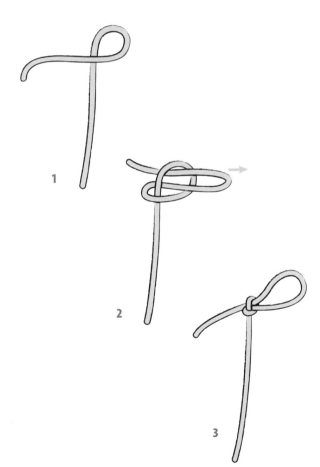

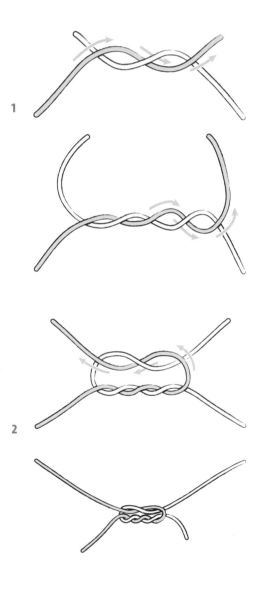

Marbled Splendor

These beads seem to combine the look of turquoise and aged brass, which can be seen in many lovely styles from Nepal and Tibet.

You will need...

5 28x18mm acrylic barrel beads with turquoise marbled finish

5 10mm matte black onyx rondelle beads

10 6mm antiqued gold-color metal rondelle spacer beads

12 inches (30 cm) .8mm clear elastic cord

All you do is...

1   Tie a slipknot on one end of the cord.

2   Thread beads in the following pattern and repeat 5 times:

1 6mm gold metal rondelle bead

1 10mm black onyx bead

1 6mm gold metal rondelle bead

1 marbled barrel bead

3   Pull out slipknot, tie a surgeon's knot, and glue. Thread one tail of cord back through marbled barrel bead and pull until knot pops into bead. Trim excess cord.

Cinnabar Magic

For centuries the Chinese mixed the mineral cinnabar with lacquer in the making of all sorts of decorative and practical objects. Cinnabar is toxic and no longer in use, but the look is simulated though the use of polymers and resins, so we can still enjoy these prettily carved beads and pendants.

You will need...

7 17mm carved flat round red cinnabar beads

18 inches (45 cm) black curb chain (10x6mm links —approx. 15 links/10 cm)

12 inches (30 cm) .8mm black elastic cord

All you do is...

1   Form a slipknot at one end of the cord.

2   Cut black chain into 7 lengths of 10 links.

3   Thread on 1 flat red bead. Thread on 10 links of black chain by weaving the cord in through one link and out the other.

4   Repeat step 3 until all chain and beads are used.

5   Pull out slipknot, tie a surgeon's knot, and glue. When dry, trim excess cord.

Turquoise Cuff

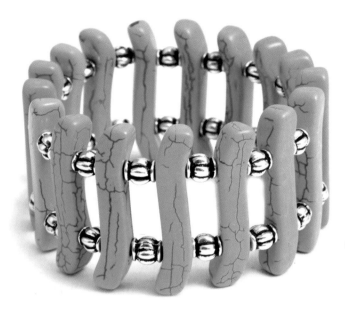

Turquoise comes in many hues, from the bright sky blue we usually associate with this stone to greenish, even yellowish, tones. It's a favorite in the jewelry of China, Tibet, India and other parts of the East.

All you do is...

1   Cut the cord into 2 12-inch (30.5 cm) pieces. Tie a slipknot at one end of each.

2   Thread one cord through the top hole of a turquoise slider then through a silver metal bead. Continue threading through the top hole of turquoise beads with a silver bead between each.

3   Pull out slipknot, tie a surgeon's knot, and glue.

4   Thread one tail of cord back through the silver metal bead and pull until knot pops into bead. Trim excess cord.

5   Repeat steps 2 through 3 for the bottom holes of the turquoise sliders (see diagram below).

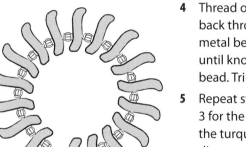

You will need...

17 5x30mm turquoise 2-hole slider beads

34 5x4mm antiqued silver metal beads

24 inches (61 cm) .8mm clear elastic cord

Classy Ceramic

The large beads are what give this bracelet its Asian flavor— a bit of calligraphy, complete with a bright red stamp.

All you do is...

1 Cut the cord into 5 14-inch (36 cm) pieces. Tie a slipknot at one end of each.

2 On one piece of cord, thread beads in the following pattern and repeat 6 times.

   1 white seed bead

   10 black seed beads

   1 white seed bead

   1 hand painted ceramic bead

3 Pull out slipknot; tie a surgeon's knot and glue.

4 Pass your next cord through a ceramic bead. Thread your seed beads in the same pattern as step 2, then pass your cord through the next ceramic bead, as shown.

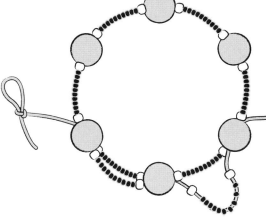

5 Continue this pattern until you reach your starting ceramic bead. Pull out slipknot; tie a surgeon's knot and glue.

6 Repeat with remaining 3 strands of cord, resulting in 5 strands of seed beads between each ceramic bead.

7 Be sure all knots have been glued, thread one tail of each strand of cord back through the ceramic bead and pull until knot pops into bead. Trim excess cord.

You will need...

6 12mm round hand painted ceramic beads with holes should be large enough to accommodate 5 .8mm strands

60 6/0 opaque white seed beads

360 11/0 opaque black seed beads

70 inches (about 1.8 m) .8mm black elastic cord strand

Exquisite Pearls

Pearls have been a mainstay of Asian jewelry for thousands of years. They come in many sizes and shapes, and in shades from purest white to pale pink to rainbow-hued. They add a little elegance to every project. It's hard to go wrong with them.

You will need...

12 8mm deep pink glass pearl beads

36 8mm pale pink glass pearl beads

36 8mm cream glass pearl beads

6 10x6mm clear faceted glass rondelle beads

12 10x6mm silver faceted glass rondelle beads

3 12x10mm clear faceted glass rondelle beads

3 10mm clear faceted bicone beads

108 11/0 silver seed beads

108 silver-colored head pins

14 inches (36 cm) .8mm clear elastic cord

All you do is...

1 Make a slipknot on one end of your cord and set aside.

2 Onto each head pin thread a silver seed bead (not pictured in diagram) followed by a pearl or rondelle or bicone bead.

3 Use flat nose pliers to bend the wire at a right angle, keeping the bend as close the bead as you can.

4 Using round nose pliers, start at one end and roll the wire around one barrel of the pliers, forming a coil until it stops at the bead.

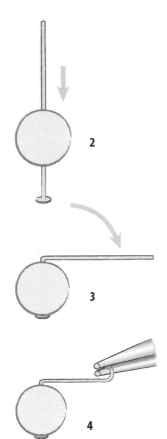

5 When all bead units have been completed thread them onto the elastic cord (with a slipknot at one end) in the following order:

a. **1 pale pink pearl**

b. **1 cream pearl**

c. **1 pale pink pearl**

d. **1 small clear rondelle**

e. **1 cream pearl**

f. **1 pale pink pearl**

g. **1 cream pearl**

h. **1 silver rondelle**

i. **1 deep pink pearl**

j. **1 pale pink pearl**

k. **1 cream pearl**

l. **1 pale pink pearl**

m. **1 large clear rondelle**

n. **1 cream pearl**

o. **1 pale pink pearl**

p. **1 cream pearl**

q. **1 silver rondelle**

r. **1 deep pink pearl**

6 Repeat step 5, but substitute the large clear rondelle bead (m) with the faceted bicone.

7 Repeat steps 5 and 6 two more times, arranging the beads so the fullness is distributed.

HINT
See Chapter 5 to learn the simple, single-loop method of making dangles.

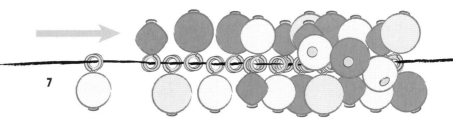

8 Pull out slipknot; tie a surgeon's knot and glue. When dry, trim excess cord.

Jade & Onyx Watch Band

Nothing says Asian style more clearly than jade. Confucius attributed to jade such virtues as purity, justice and intelligence. Here, this timeless stone transforms a timepiece into an elegant bracelet.

You will need...

10 12mm round jade beads

6 15x20mm antiqued silver-plated beads

12 10mm matte black onyx rondelle beads

20 antiqued silver-plated decorative bead caps

4 3mm round silver-plated beads

4 15mm lobster clasps

24 inches (61 cm) 1mm clear elastic cord

1 watch face with watchband bars – 35x40mm

5 Repeat steps 2, 3 and 4.

All you do is...

1 Make a slipknot at one end of your cord.

2 Thread on in the following order:

    a. 1 black onyx bead

    b. 1 large silver bead

    c. 1 black onyx bead

    d. 1 silver bead cap

    e. 1 jade bead

    f. 1 silver bead cap

3 Repeat twice more.

4 Continue by threading on in the following order:

    a. 1 small silver bead

    b. 1 lobster clasp

    c. 1 silver bead cap

    d. 1 jade bead

    e. 1 silver bead cap

    f. 1 lobster clasp (facing the same way as the previous lobster clasp)

    g. 1 small silver bead

    h. 1 silver bead cap

    i. 1 jade bead

    j. 1 silver bead cap

6 Pull out slipknot and remove the first black onyx bead from step 2 and thread it onto the end of beads from step 5 (you are just transferring it from the beginning of the strand to the end of the strand).

7 Tie a surgeon's knot and glue. Thread one tail of cord back through the large silver metal bead and pull until knot pops into bead. Trim excess cord.

8 Attach beaded band to watch band bar using the lobster clasps. (Since the watch is removable, try making a few different bands for it!)

CHAPTER 2
Memory Wire Jewelry

Using Memory Wire

Memory wire is a fun and easy yet effective way to create gorgeous jewelry pieces. The metal wire is formed into continuous rings that hold their shape. Memory wire is available in a variety of sizes for creating necklaces, bracelets and rings.

Tools for working with memory wire

Memory wire cutters/shears

Wire cutters (for cutting eye and head pins when making dangles, NOT for cutting memory wire, as this wire is hard enough to damage ordinary cutters!)

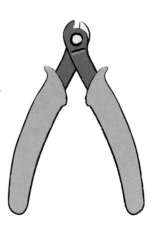

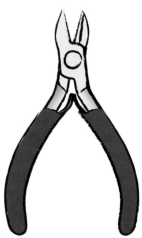

Optional extras

The looped ends of memory wire can be left as they are or they can be decorated with bead dangles that you make by threading beads onto a head pin and forming a simple loop.

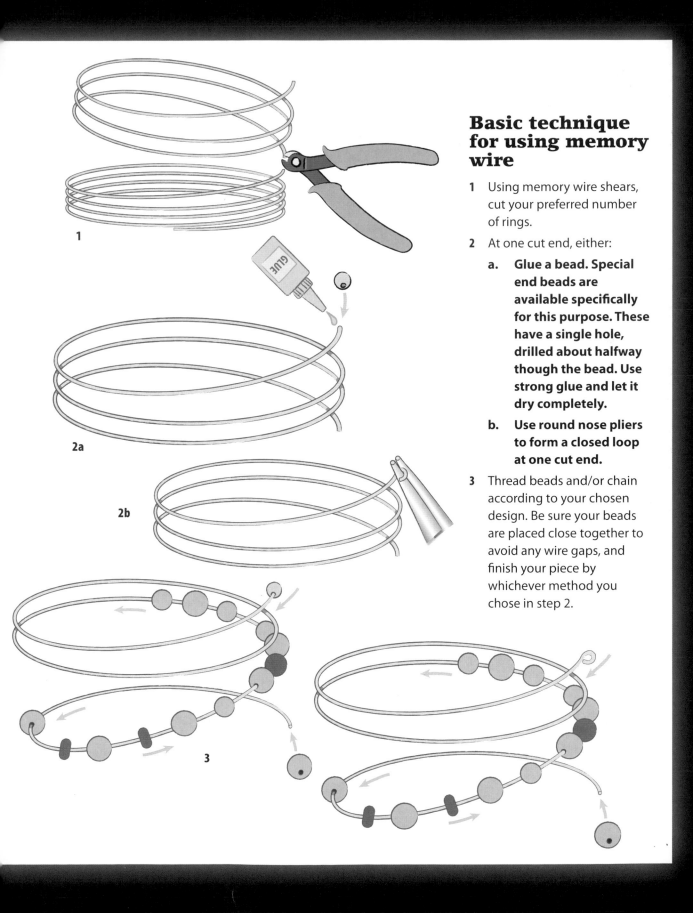

Basic technique for using memory wire

1 Using memory wire shears, cut your preferred number of rings.

2 At one cut end, either:

   a. **Glue a bead. Special end beads are available specifically for this purpose. These have a single hole, drilled about halfway though the bead. Use strong glue and let it dry completely.**

   b. **Use round nose pliers to form a closed loop at one cut end.**

3 Thread beads and/or chain according to your chosen design. Be sure your beads are placed close together to avoid any wire gaps, and finish your piece by whichever method you chose in step 2.

1

2a

2b

GLUE

3

Hints & tips

- For a dangle with several bead units, thread bead(s) onto an eye pin instead of a head pin and form a loop. Attach one end to the memory wire loop. Make and attach a single dangle to other end.

- You may need to adjust your pattern at the end to accommodate a final bead; or, you may choose to cut off excess memory wire.

- Occasionally a larger-holed glass bead may "swallow" the seed bead next to it. If this should happen, you can use a larger seed bead or feed extra seed beads until the hole of the larger bead is full before continuing with the pattern.

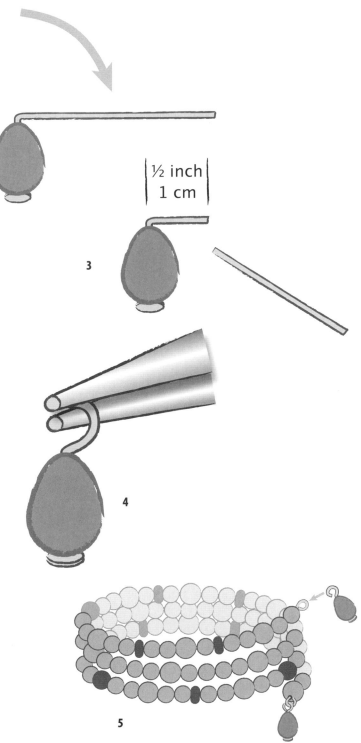

Basic technique for making dangles

1   As per the technique for making the Exquisite Pearls bracelet in chapter 1, thread a bead or two onto a head pin.

2   Using your flat nose pliers, bend the head pin at a right angle, keeping the bend as close to the bead as you can.

3   Use your cutters to trim the wire to about ½ inch (1 cm).

4   Roll the head pin wire tight around one barrel of your round nose pliers, forming a tight closed loop.

5   Dangles are a nice way to finish off a memory wire piece. To attach, use flat nose pliers to twist the loop of the dangle slightly to the side, slip onto the memory wire loop and twist closed. (See chapter 5 for more on opening and closing loops and making dangles.)

Wood & Metal Cuff

The warmth of wood has a home in all sorts of Asian styles, from carved bracelets and pendants to simple beads. This simple bracelet has a look of strings of Tibetan prayer beads—with some metal embellishments thrown in.

You will need...

memory wire – 2¼-inch stainless steel bracelet (.60-.75mm thick)

approximately 160 round 6/0 seed beads - iris bronze

approximately 64 round 6mm wood beads - dark brown

approximately 18 fluted 7mm metal rondelle beads - antiqued gold

approximately 40 round 10mm wood beads - dark brown

approximately 18 flat round 8mm rondelle beads - antiqued gold

approximately 17 round 14mm cushion bead - dark brown

4 gold-plated head pins

All you do is...

1. Cut a length of memory wire 7 rings plus 1 inch (3 cm) long.

2. Form a closed loop at one end of the memory wire, then thread beads in following pattern:

    a. **1 full ring of iris bronze 6/0 seed beads (approx. 70 beads)**

    b. **1 full ring of 6mm dark brown round wood beads, with a seed bead between every two beads**

    c. **1 full ring of 10mm dark brown round wood beads with a fluted rondelle between every two beads**

    d. **1 full ring of 14mm dark brown round wood**

    cushion beads with flat rondelles between them

    e. **1 full ring of 10mm beads with a fluted rondelle between every two beads**

    f. **1 full ring of 6mm beads with a seed bead between every two beads**

    g. **1 full ring of seed beads (approx. 70 beads)**

3. Form a closed loop at the end of the memory wire.

4. Thread a 6mm dark brown round wood bead onto a head pin and make a loop. Repeat 3 more times.

5. Attach two of the bead units from step 4 to each of the closed loops at each end of the bracelet.

Aqua Lampwork With Silver Tubes

This bracelet was inspired by the lavish use of silver, the deep blue of sapphires and the aqua tints of chalcedony that can be seen in a lot of the jewelry of India.

You will need...

memory wire – 2¼-inch stainless steel bracelet (.60-.75mm thick)

32 round 11/0 seed beads - silver metallic

28 flat round (abacus-shaped) 4x6mm beads - sparkling silver

12 round 3mm beads - dark aqua

8 round 8mm lampwork beads - aqua

10 round 6mm beads - dark aqua

5 round 10x14mm lampwork beads - aqua

10 30x4mm curved metal tubes - silver-plated

6 silver-colored head pins

All you do is...

1 Cut a length of memory wire 3 rings plus 3 inches (6 cm) long.

2 Form a closed loop at one end of the memory wire, then thread beads in the following pattern:

   1 seed bead, 1 sparkling silver bead, 1 seed bead

   1 3mm dark aqua bead and 1 seed bead

   1 sparkling silver bead, 1 8mm aqua lampwork bead, 1 sparkling silver bead

   1 seed bead, 1 3mm dark aqua bead, 1 seed bead

   1 sparkling silver bead, 1 curved silver tube

   1 6mm dark aqua bead, 1 10x14mm aqua lampwork bead, 1 6mm dark aqua bead

   1 sparkling silver bead

3 Repeat pattern 4 times and finish with:

   1 4x6mm sparkling silver bead & 1 silver seed bead

   1 dark aqua 3mm bead & 1 silver seed bead

   1 4x6mm sparkling silver bead, 1 8mm aqua lampwork bead, 1 4x6mm sparkling silver bead

   1 silver seed bead, 1 dark aqua 3mm bead, 1 silver seed bead

   1 4x6mm sparkling silver bead & 1 silver seed bead.

4 Form a closed loop at the end of the memory wire.

5 Thread a silver seed bead then a 4x6mm sparkling silver bead onto a head pin and make a loop. Repeat 3 more times.

6 Thread a seed bead followed by an 8mm lampwork bead and then another seed bead and make a loop. Repeat once more.

7 Attach 2 sparkling silver bead units (step 5) and a lampwork bead unit (step 6) to the closed loop at each end of the bracelet.

Jade, Flowers & Butterflies

Even in chip form, natural stones form a beautiful base for bracelets and necklaces. In this bracelet, natural jade is enhanced by charms of a style that can be seen on simple Asian-style fabric prints.

You will need...

memory wire – 2¼inch stainless steel bracelet (.60-.75mm thick)

approximately 100 round 11/0 seed beads-gold metallic

20 6mm antiqued gold flower beads (I have used two different designs)

22 4x6mm antiqued gold rondelle beads

9x11mm antiqued gold butterfly beads

approximately 66 small jade chips/nuggets

13 gold-plated head pins

11 gold-plated 4mm jump rings

4 gold-plated eye pins

All you do is...

1   Cut a length of memory wire 3 full rings plus 2½ inches (6 cm) long.

2   Form a closed loop at one end the of memory wire.

3   Make 6 flower charms by threading a flower bead onto a head pin and making a loop. Attach to a 4mm jump ring.

4   Make 6 butterfly charms by threading a gold seed bead, a butterfly bead and another seed bead onto a head pin and making a loop. Attach to a 4mm jump ring.

5   Thread beads onto the memory wire in the following pattern:

a.   seed bead
b.   flower bead
c.   seed bead
d.   jade chip
e.   seed bead
f.   jade chip
g.   seed bead
h.   jade chip
i.   seed bead
j.   rondelle bead
k.   flower charm
l.   rondelle bead
m.   seed bead
n.   jade chip
o.   seed bead
p.   jade chip
q.   seed bead
r.   jade chip
s.   seed bead
t.   flower bead
u.   seed bead
v.   jade chip
w.   seed bead
x.   jade chip
y.   seed bead
z.   jade chip
aa.   seed bead
bb.   rondelle bead
cc.   butterfly charm
dd.   rondelle bead
ee.   seed bead
ff.   jade chip
gg.   seed bead
hh.   jade chip
ii.   seed bead
jj.   jade chip

6 Repeat step 5 four more times.

7 Finish with:

    a. **seed bead**

    b. **flower bead**

    c. **seed bead**

    d. **jade chip**

    e. **seed bead**

    f. **jade chip**

    g. **seed bead**

    h. **jade chip**

    i. **seed bead**

    j. **rondelle bead**

    k. **flower charm**

    l. **rondelle bead**

    m. **seed bead**

    n. **jade chip**

    o. **seed bead**

    p. **jade chip**

    q. **seed bead**

    r. **jade chip**

    s. **seed bead**

    t. **flower bead**

    u. **seed bead**

8 Thread onto an eye pin a gold seed bead, a butterfly bead and a gold seed bead. Form a loop. Repeat with a second eye pin.

9 Thread 3 jade chips onto an eye pin and form a loop. Repeat.

10 Thread a flower charm onto a head pin and form a loop. Repeat.

11 Attach the flower from step 10 to one loop of the jade chips from step 9. Attach the butterfly from step 8 to the other loop of the jade chips. Repeat.

12 Attach the butterfly end of each completed dangle to the loop at each end of the bracelet.

Black Velvet Choker

This elegant choker features one of the many round patterns seen on vases, fabrics and carvings of the Far East.

All you do is...

1   Cut a length of memory wire 1 ring plus 1 inch (3 cm) long.

2   Cut 4 pieces of velvet/velour tubing, each at just under ½ inch (12 mm) long. For a larger choker you may wish to cut longer pieces – adjust size as needed.

3   Thread a gold puff bead onto memory wire, letting it fall to the center.

4   Thread on either side of the bead:

   a.   1 12mm round glass bead

   b.   1 puff bead

5   Apply a thin coat of G-S Hypo Cement to about 10 mm of memory wire next to the gold puff beads placed at the end of step 3. Thread on a length of tubing over the adhesive. Push the tubing tight against the gold puff bead and allow to dry.

6   Thread next to tubing on either side of necklace:

   a.   1 drum bead

   b.   1 rondelle

   c.   1 disc bead

   d.   1 rondelle

   e.   1 drum bead

7   Apply a thin coat of G-S Hypo Cement to a bit less than ¼ inch (10 mm) of memory wire next to the last gold drum bead from step 6. Thread a length of tubing over the adhesive. Push the tubing tight against the gold drum bead. Allow to dry.

8   Repeat step 6.

9   Cut 2 pieces of tubing to fit the remaining memory wire, less about 2 mm (you'll need to keep the ends of the wire clear for applying the end beads).

10 Apply a thin coat of G-S Hypo Cement to a bit less than ¼ inch (10 mm) of memory wire next to the gold drum bead placed in step 8.

11 Thread tubing onto remaining exposed memory wire and over the adhesive from step 10 next to the gold drum bead. Allow to dry.

12 Use G-S Hypo Cement to glue the end beads to wire ends as close to the tubing as possible. Allow to set and dry completely.

You will need...

memory wire – gold-color necklace size

approximately 7 inches (18 cm) 3mm velvet/velour tubing - black

8 6x8mm drum beads - antiqued gold

8 round flat 10mm rondelle beads - matte black onyx

4 round flat 10mm disc beads - shiny gold

3 12x12mm etched puff bead - antiqued gold

2 12mm round glass bead - black

2 round 5mm end beads

adhesive - G-S Hypo Cement

Red Fossil Coral Choker

Faceted, smooth, or in chip form, carnelian is a gorgeous complement to red as well as to metals of all kinds. Once thought to protect the wearer from evil, it can be found in jewelry from all over Asia, from ancient amulets and headdresses to the most contemporary jewelry designs.

All you do is...

1   Cut two lengths of necklace memory wire sufficient to encircle the base of the neck plus approximately 2 inches (5 cm). Each wire should be between 17¾-19 inches (45-50 cm) long. One should be slightly longer than the other.

2   Form a closed loop at one end of the shorter length of wire. Thread beads in following pattern:

   a.   **1 small gold bead**

   b.   **the top hole of a coral bead**

   c.   **1 small gold bead**

   d.   **1 inch (2 cm) of carnelian chips (the number will depend on the size and shape, about 4-5)**

3   Repeat 8 times.

4   Finish with:

   a.   **1 small gold bead**

   b.   **one hole of a double drilled red fossil coral bead**

   c.   **1 small gold bead**

5   Form a closed loop at the end.

6   Form a closed loop at one end of the longer length of wire. Thread beads in the following pattern:

   a.   **1 small gold bead**

   b.   **the bottom hole of the coral bead strung directly above**

   c.   **1 small gold bead**

   d.   **enough carnelian chips to ensure that the next gold bead will be even with the one above it. (The bottom strand needs to be slightly longer than the top strand in order for the necklace to lie flat, so you may need to add an extra chip or two each time you perform this step.)**

7   Repeat 8 times.

8   Finish with:

   a.   **1 small gold bead**

   b.   **remaining hole of the last coral bead**

   c.   **1 small gold bead**

9   Form a closed loop at the end.

10 Pass a jump ring through the two loops at one end of the necklace.

11 Pass a jump ring with a lobster clasp through the two loops at the other end of the necklace.

You will need...

memory wire – gold-color necklace size

10 double drilled 10x20mm rectangular red fossil coral beads

approximately 100 carnelian chips (depending on size)

40 round 4mm beads - gold

2 9mm jump rings - gold

1 12x6mm lobster clasp - gold

Silver & Jet Ring

This ring is a salute to the many ways cool silver and black stone have been combined in Asian jewelry. The dullish silver of these seed beads would set off any dark-colored beads to stunning effect.

You will need:

memory wire – ¾-inch ring size

approximately 230 11/0 seed beads - silver metallic

3 ball-end head pin-silver

2 4mm faceted bicone beads - jet

1 6mm faceted bicone bead - jet

2 3mm faceted round bead - jet

2 4mm crystal and silver-plated rondelle

3 silver ball head pins

All you do is...

1   Cut a length of memory wire 5 rings long.

2   Form a closed loop at one end of the memory wire.

3   Fill all 5 rings of memory wire with silver seed beads.

4   Form a closed loop at the other end of the memory wire.

5   Pass a silver ball-end head pin through one loop at the end of the memory wire.

6   Onto the head pin thread 1 small jet bicone, 1 crystal and silver rondelle, 1 medium jet bicone, the other rondelle and the other small jet bicone.

7   Pass the ball-end head pin through the closed loop at the other end of the memory wire and form a loop.

8   Thread a faceted round jet faceted bead onto a silver ball-head pin and form a loop. Repeat with another round jet faceted bead.

9   Attach the two small jet faceted beads to the loop at the end of the ball-end head pin.

Black & Pink Sparkle Ring

Black and pink are often combined in Asian aesthetics—pink peonies on a black cloisonne dish, a black yukata with pink obi, and beautiful black hair adorned with a single pink flower are all inspirations for this ring.

All you do is...

1. Cut a length of memory wire 5 rings long.

2. Use G-S Hypo Cement to glue one end bead to one end of the memory wire. Allow to set and dry thoroughly.

3. Fill 2⅓ rings of memory wire with black seed beads.

4. Thread on the following pattern:

   a. 1 silver seed bead, 1 4mm fuchsia bicone, 1 silver seed bead

   b. 5 mm black crystal bicone

   c. 1 silver seed bead, 1 4mm fuchsia bicone, 1 silver seed bead

5. Fill the remainder of the memory wire with black seed beads.

6. Use G-S Hypo Cement to glue end bead to end of the memory wire. Allow to set and dry thoroughly.

You will need...

memory wire – ¾-inch ring size

approximately 210 11/0 seed beads - black

4 11/0 seed beads - silver metallic

2 4mm faceted bicone - fuchsia

1 5mm faceted bicone - black

2 round 3mm half drilled end beads for memory wire - silver

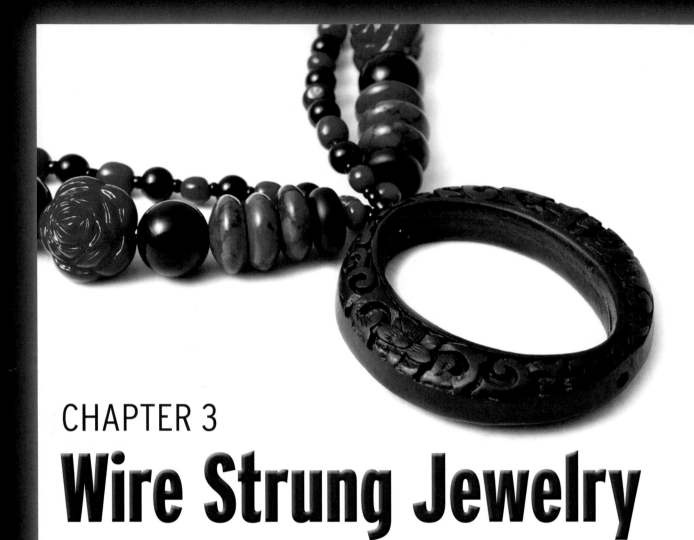

CHAPTER 3
Wire Strung Jewelry

Using Beading Wire and Crimp Beads

One of my favorite stringing techniques is the use of beading wire and crimp beads. Today's beading wires provide a wide range of strength and flexibility that I often find is more durable than traditional beading threads. It is quick and easy, which is a bonus for beginners and experienced beaders alike! Wire also comes in different thicknesses and colors, making it possible for exposed wire to be an attractive part of the design. Crimps come in bead or tube form and are available in many sizes. Be sure to choose the bead or tube that best suits the thickness of your beading wire. Be sure to take into account how many strands will ultimately pass through the crimp.

Attaching a clasp using the flat crimp technique

1 Thread a crimp bead onto beading wire, followed by one side of the clasp.

2 Thread end of beading wire back through crimp bead, forming a loop around clasp.

3 Pull tail until loop is tight around clasp. Leave about a 1-inch (2 cm) tail.

4 Hold crimp between jaws of flat nose pliers and squeeze firmly to flatten and set crimp bead.

5 Pull firmly on wire to check crimp is secure (if wire slips, repeat technique with a new crimp bead).

6 Thread on beads in your chosen pattern, with the first few beads passing over the 1-inch (2 cm) tail.

7 Thread a crimp bead onto beading wire, followed by the other side of the clasp.

8 Thread end of beading wire back through crimp bead (and, if possible, through the last few beads of the piece), forming a loop around clasp.

9 Hold the clasp while pulling the tail in order to avoid any visible wire gaps between beads, or between the beads and the clasp.

10 When satisfied, squeeze crimp bead and cut excess wire.

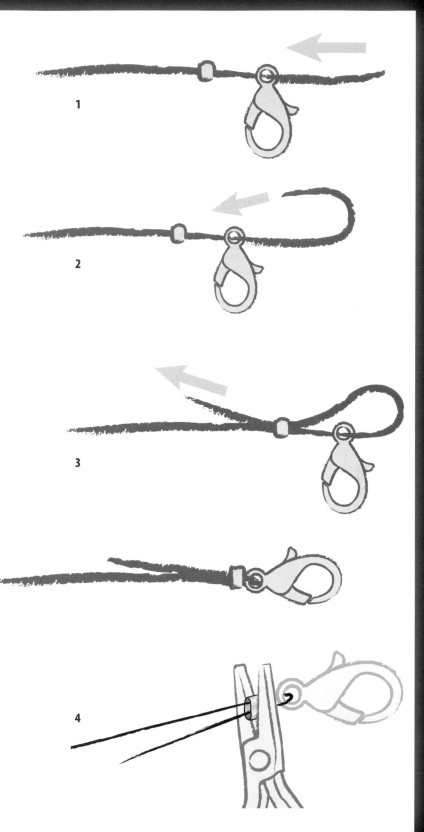

The folded crimp technique

For this technique you'll need a crimping tool.
The half-moon notch (generally the bottom notch)
will create a separate chamber for each strand,
forming a U-shaped crimp. The smaller notch will fold
the two chambers together, tightening the crimp.

1 Follow steps 1-3 of the flat crimp technique.
2 Position crimp bead into half moon
   notch, ensuring that the strands are
   separated, and squeeze firmly,
   resulting in a U-shaped crimp.
3 Turn the crimp over onto its side and
   place in the round notch of pliers.
4 Squeeze and fold crimp in half at the
   indentation.

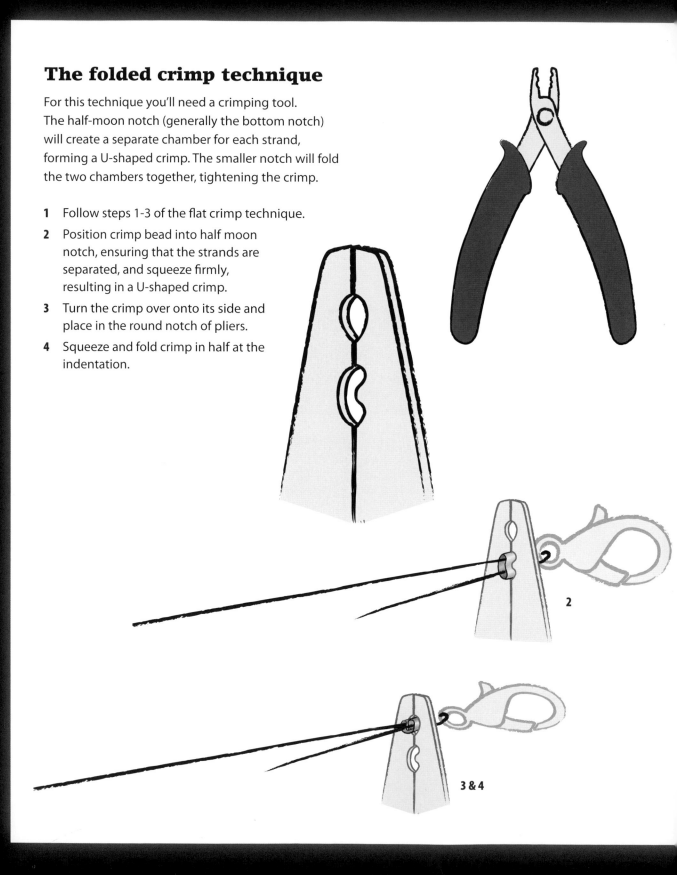

2

3 & 4

When to use flat or folded crimping techniques

Either flat or folded crimps are acceptable for making all manner of jewelry. Basically it comes down to preference. You may prefer to use the folded technique if the crimp bead is going to be noticeable.

For attaching clasps or whenever a secure connection is required, I prefer the flat technique. A crimp cover can be used to hide the flattened crimp bead.

Floating beads on beading wire using crimp beads

When floating beads on a single strand, it's best to choose the smallest crimp bead the strand—and the size of the floating bead—can accommodate, especially if the design is too tight for using crimp covers. A small crimp bead will respond best to the flat crimp technique. Whichever technique you choose, use just enough pressure to hold your bead in place. Over-crimping weakens the crimp bead.

1 Thread a crimp bead onto beading wire and crimp just about where you'd like your bead to rest.

2 Thread your bead(s) followed by a second crimp bead.

3 Use pliers to push second crimp bead close to bead and crimp.

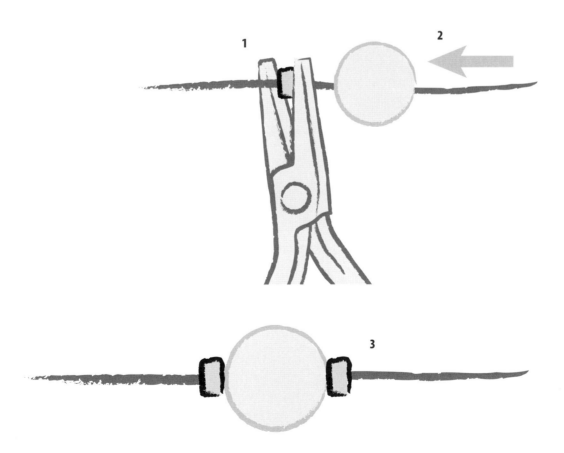

Etched Jade Necklace

This choker shows how a terrific focal piece and great accents can make the easiest project a thing of beauty.

All you do is...

1 Using the flat crimp technique, attach the lobster clasp to one end of the wire.

2 Thread beads in the following pattern:

   a. 1 seed bead

   b. 1 bead cap

   c. 1 chrysoprase tube

   d. 1 rondelle

   e. Repeat c and d twice more

   f. 1 gold tube

   g. 1 rondelle

   h. Repeat c and d twice

   i. Repeat f though h

   j. Repeat f and g

   k. Repeat c and d

   l. 1 chrysoprase tube

3 Thread a seed bead, a bead cap, the jade focal bead, another bead cap and another seed bead.

4 Thread beads up the other side of the focal bead to mirror the beads threaded in step 2.

5 Finish by attaching the jump ring to end of beading wire.

You will need...

gold-colored beading wire –24 inches (60 cm)

2 gold crimp beads

18x40mm etched jade focal bead

18 8x11mm chrysoprase tube beads

6 6x8mm antiqued gold-plated tube beads

22 4x6mm gold-plated faceted rondelle beads

4 11/0 gold metallic seed beads

4 10mm fancy gold bead caps

7mm gold-plated jump ring

12mm gold-plated lobster clasp

Blue & Jade Necklace

Japan and China have always decked themselves in shades of blue—the indigo of Japanese cottons and origami papers and the many shades of Chinese porcelain, from softest washes of color to the deepest shades of cobalt and lapis. Add to that touches of jade and you have a lovely tribute to Asian influence. Both necklace and earrings show how different colors of stringing wire can be part of the design, and part of the fun.

You will need. . .

55 inches (140 cm) aqua blue beading wire

55 inches (140 cm) lime green beading wire

55 inches (140 cm) shiny silver beading wire

6 silver crimp beads

2 3-strand spacer ends

3 5mm silver-plated jump rings

6 silver crimp covers

1 silver lobster clasp

1 extender chain

1 silver swirl pendant

8 15mm round blue & green swirl porcelain beads

16 4x6mm antiqued pewter spacer beads

4 3x4mm antiqued pewter spacer beads

2 5x5mm antiqued silver-plated metal spacer tubes

7 6mm antiqued metal flower beads (add a flower bead to the end of the extender chain)

6 8x10mm deep blue faceted glass beads

6 8x10 light blue faceted glass beads

6 4x6mm dark blue faceted glass beads

18 small jade chips

This project utilizes crimp covers. These clever disguises look like basic spacer beads. They come in gold, silver, even copper and bronze tones, and in finishes from shiny to antiqued, as well as in several sizes.

To use them, just slip the open end around your crimp bead and gently squeeze closed with flat nosed pliers or the small notch of your crimping tool.

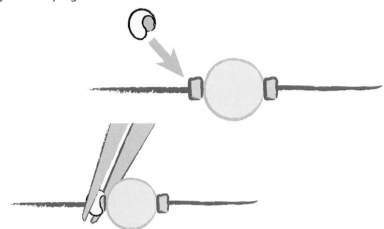

All you do is...

1   Attach a jump ring to swirl pendant and set aside.

2   Cut two 27½-inch (70 mm) strands each of aqua, lime and shiny silver beading wire

3   Use the flat crimp technique to attach the two lengths of aqua beading wire to one loop of one 3-loop spacer end. Repeat with lime and shiny silver beading wire strands.

4   Cover the flat crimps with silver crimp covers.

5   Thread all 6 strands of beading wire through 4x6mm antiqued pewter spacer bead, 1 15mm blue and green swirl porcelain bead and another 4x6mm antiqued pewter spacer bead.

6   Thread three strands of wire (1 aqua, 1 lime and 1 silver) through an 8x10mm deep blue faceted glass bead then thread the following beads, each on a separate strand of beading wire:

   a.   **1 antiqued metal flower bead**

   b.   **1 4x6mm dark blue faceted glass bead**

   c.   **1 small jade chip**

7   Take the other three strands of wire (1 aqua, 1 lime and 1 silver) and thread the following beads, each on a separate strand of beading wire:

   a.   **1 antiqued 5x5mm silver-plated metal spacer tube**

   b.   **2 jade chips**

8 Thread three strands from step 6 through 8x10mm light blue faceted glass bead.

9 Stagger the beads from steps 5-7 before passing all the strands of wire through a pewter spacer bead, a 15mm blue and green swirl porcelain bead and another pewter spacer bead.

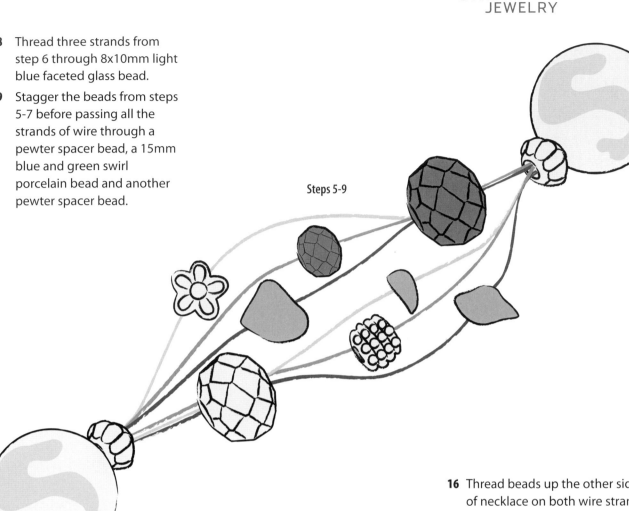

Steps 5-9

10 Thread three strands of wire (1 aqua, 1 lime and 1 silver) through an 8x10mm deep blue faceted glass bead then thread the following beads, each on a separate strand of beading wire:

   a. **4x6mm dark blue faceted glass bead**

   b. **1 antiqued metal flower bead**

   c. **1 small jade chip**

11 Thread the other three strands of wire (1 aqua, 1 lime and 1 silver) and thread the following beads, each on a separate strand of beading wire:

   a. **1 antiqued 3x4mm pewter spacer bead**

   b. **2 small jade chips**

12 Thread the three strands from step 10 through an 8x10mm light blue faceted glass bead.

13 Repeat steps 8 through 11.

14 Repeat step 5.

15 Thread all six strands through jump ring attached to silver swirl pendant.

16 Thread beads up the other side of necklace on both wire strands, to mirror the beads placed in steps 5 through 14).

17 Using the flat crimp technique, attach the two strands of each color of beading wire to one of the loops of the 3-strand spacer end.

18 Use a jump ring to attach the lobster clasp to the 3-strand spacer end.

19 Use a jump ring to attach the extender chain to the other 3-strand spacer end.

20 Thread a flower bead onto an antiqued silver metal flower bead and form a loop. Attach to the end of the extender chain.

Elegant Earrings

A lovely complement to the Blue & Jade Necklace, these earrings show how a basic design and a few beads of varying tone, size and shape can be all you need to make a statement.

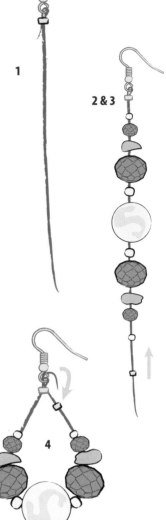

You will need. . .

8 inches (20 cm) aqua blue beading wire

4 silver crimp beads

2 silver crimp bead covers

8 11/0 silver seed beads

4 small jade chips

4 4x6mm light blue faceted beads

4 8x10mm dark blue faceted beads

2 15mm round blue and green swirl porcelain beads

2 silver-plated ear wires

All you do is. . .

1 Cut the wire in half so that you have two 4-inch (10 cm) lengths and, using the flat crimp technique, attach the end of one length to the loop of one ear wire.

2 Thread on the following beads.

   a. 1 seed bead

   b. 1 4x6mm light blue faceted bead

   c. 1 jade chip

   d. 1 8x10mm dark blue faceted bead

   e. 1 seed bead

   f. 1 15mm porcelain bead.

3 Thread beads up the other side of earring to mirror those in a to e above.

4 Use the flat crimp technique to attach the other end to the loop of the ear wire.

5 Holding both crimps together, cover with a silver crimp cover.

6 Repeat to make second earring.

Coral & Lava Bracelet

Bamboo coral is often dyed to give it the bright flame color that comes naturally to some other types of coral. In this bracelet, glossy coral makes a strong contrast to porous lava—another fun red-and-black combo, enhanced by cool silver.

You will need...

24 inches (60 cm) black beading wire

4 small silver crimp beads

7 30x10mm (approx.) red coral stems, double drilled

16 10mm black lava beads

1 6mm red coral bead

1 silver-plated head pin

1 11/0 black seed bead

2 double strand antique pewter end bar

8 7mm silver-plated jump rings

1 5mm silver-plated jump ring

1 large (approx. 22mm) silver-plated lobster clasp

All you do is...

1   Cut wire in half and, using the flat crimp technique, attach one strand to each of the loops of one end bar.

2   Thread beading wire through one lava bead then through one end of coral stem. Repeat until you have 8 lava beads and 7 coral stems. Fold a piece of masking tape or similar over the end of the strand.

3   Repeat step 2 on the other strand of beading wire.

4   Using the flat crimp technique, attach each strand of beading wire to the corresponding loop of the second end bar.

5   Make an extender chain by attaching the 7mm jump rings to each other.

6   Thread a small black seed bead and a small round coral bead on the head pin and make a loop. Attach to one end of the extender chain.

7   Attach the other end of the extender chain to one end bar.

8   Use a 5mm jump ring to attach the lobster clasp to the other end bar.

From the whimsical netsuke of Japan to the most elegant elaborate carvings from China, ivory has long been a prized component of much of Asian art. Now, as a part of wildlife protection, other materials of similar tint, including wood, glass and porcelain, are used in its stead. The Asian-style butterfly motif of the pendant and the soft glow of the pearls lend a vintage look to this necklace.

You will need...

1 carved ivory-toned pendant

27½ inches (70 cm) gold beading wire

20 small gold crimp beads

16 glitter gold crimp covers

24 8mm (approx.) freshwater pearls

24 11/0 gold metallic seed beads

8 6x8mm faceted crystal beads

2 8x10mm AB faceted crystal beads

1 7mm gold-plated jump ring

1 12mm gold-plated lobster clasp

All you do is...

1 Using the flat crimp technique, attach the lobster clasp to one end of the wire.

2 Thread on a freshwater pearl and a gold crimp bead and use flat crimp technique to hold the pearl tight against the flattened crimp bead from step 1.

3 Squeeze a crimp bead ½ inch (1 cm) from this second crimp

4 Thread beads in the following pattern:

   a.   **1 freshwater pearl**

   b.   **1 11/0 gold metallic seed bead**

   c.   **6x8mm faceted crystal bead**

   d.   **1 gold metallic seed bead**

   e.   **1 freshwater pearl**

   f.   **1 crimp bead**

5 Push the beads up against the crimp bead from step 3. Using the flat technique, squeeze the crimp bead you added at the end of step 4.

6 Squeeze a crimp bead 1 inch (2 cm) from the crimp bead in step 5.

7 Thread beads in the following pattern:

   a.   **1 freshwater pearl**

   b.   **1 11/0 gold metallic seed bead**

   c.   **6x8mm faceted crystal bead**

   d.   **1 gold metallic seed bead**

   e.   **1 freshwater pearl**

   f.   **1 11/0 gold metallic seed bead**

   g.   **1 8x10mm AB faceted crystal bead**

   h.   **1 11/0 gold metallic seed bead**

   i.   **Repeat a through e**

   j.   **1 crimp bead**

8 Push the beads up against the crimp bead from step 6. Using the flat technique, squeeze the crimp bead you added at the end of step 7.

9 Squeeze a crimp bead 1 inch (2 cm) from the previous crimp bead in step 8.

10 Repeat steps 4 and 5.

11 Squeeze a crimp bead 1 inch (2 cm) from the previous crimp bead.

12 Attach jump ring to pendant. Set aside.

13 Thread beads in the following pattern:

   a.   **1 freshwater pearl, 1 gold seed bead, 1 freshwater pearl, 1 gold seed bead, 1 freshwater pearl**

   b.   **the jump ring attached to pendant**

   c.   **Repeat a**

   d.   **1 crimp bead**

14 Push the beads up against the crimp bead from step 11. Using the flat technique, squeeze the crimp bead you added at the end of step 13.

15 Thread beads up the other side of necklace to mirror the beads placed in steps 2 through 11.

16 Using the flat crimp technique, attach the jump ring to end of beading wire.

17 Finish by covering all the crimp beads with gold glitter crimp covers (except for the two flat crimp beads holding the clasp in place).

Red & Black Double Strand Cinnabar Necklace

Red and black together bring to mind beautiful Chinese lacquerware and the glossy black hair and red lips of the Japanese geisha.

HINT

Remember that, especially when making multiple-strand necklaces, following the metric measurements will give you more accurate proportions, which can result in better drape.

All you do is...

1. Cut the beading wire in half and, using the flat crimp technique, attach the hook of the clasp to one end of both lengths of beading wire.

1

2. Thread both strands through a 6mm black glass bead.

3. Thread beads onto the outside strand of wire in the following pattern (creates a string of beads approximately 9¼ inches [23.5 cm] long):

   a. **1 11/0 black seed bead**

   b. **3 4x14mm red coral rondelle beads**

   c. **1 18x6mm flat black cinnabar bead**

   d. **Repeat b**

   e. **1 12mm round black glass bead**

   f. **1 15x18mm red flower bead**

   g. **Repeat f**

   h. **Repeat b to g**

   i. **Repeat b**

   j.

   k.

   l. **Repeat a**

4. On the inside strand of wire create a string of alternating red coral beads and 6mm black glass beads with an 11/0 black seed bead between each and finishing with 3 black seed beads (creates a strand of beads approximately 8 inches [20 cm] long)

5. Thread both strands of beading wire through the hole at one end of the black cinnabar pendant, through a 11/0 black seed bead, then back through the hole in the pendant.

6. Thread beads up the other side

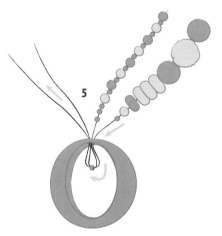

5

of necklace on both wire strands, to mirror the beads strung in steps 2 through 4.

7. Using the flat crimp technique, attach the ring side of the clasp to both ends of beading wire.

You will need...

55 inches (140 cm) black beading wire

2 medium silver crimp beads

1 large black cinnabar O-shaped pendant (48mm round)

4 18x6mm flat black cinnabar beads

2 10mm matte black onyx rondelle beads

30 4x14mm red coral rondelle beads

8 12mm round black glass beads

4 15x18mm red flower beads

28 6mm round black beads

30 assorted red coral beads (between 5 & 8mm)

65 11/0 black seed beads

1 large silver S hook clasp

Turquoise & Coral Floating Necklace

In parts of India and Tibet coral is thought to have healing and protective powers. It's often partnered with turquoise. Here, paler corals are used to enhance the soft look and feel of this necklace.

You will need...

138 inches (3.5 m) shiny silver beading thread

1 coral-colored glass flower pendant

9 15mm round flat turquoise beads

21 8mm round turquoise beads

130 (approx.) 2x5mm orange coral discs

140 (approx.) small silver crimp beads

2 5-strand end bars

2 7mm silver-plated jump rings

1 lobster clasp

All you do is...

1 Cut five lengths of silver beading wire as follows: 25½ inches (65 cm), 26½ inches (67 cm), 27 inches (69 cm), 28 inches (71 cm), 31 inches (79 cm).

2 Using the flat crimp technique, attach each strand of beading wire to each loop of one of the end bars, in length size order starting with the longest on the left and finishing with the shortest on the right.

3 Cover the flattened crimp beads with crimp covers if desired or if spacing allows.

4 Using the floating bead technique, float beads on each strand as listed below, staggering the beads randomly on the beading wire strands:

a. **25 ½-inch (65 cm) strand – the finished beaded strand should measure 17 inches (43 cm) with plenty of excess wire for attaching the other end:**

5 8mm round turquoise beads

5 sets of 3 2x5mm orange coral discs

2 sets of 5 2x5mm orange coral discs

2 15mm round flat turquoise beads

b. **26 ½-inch (67 strand) – the finished beaded strand should measure 18 inches (46 cm) with plenty of excess wire for attaching the other end:**

6 sets of 2 2x5mm orange coral discs

2 sets of 3 2x5mm orange coral discs

2 sets of 5 2x5mm orange coral discs

2 8mm round turquoise beads

2 15mm round flat turquoise beads

c. **27-inch (69 cm) strand – the finished beaded strand should measure 19 inches (49 cm) with plenty of excess wire for attaching the other end:**

10 sets of 2 2x5mm orange coral discs

3 sets of 3 2x5mm orange coral discs

2 8mm round turquoise beads

d. **28-inch (71 cm) strand – the finished strand with beads on it should measure 20 inches (51 cm) with plenty of excess wire for attaching the other end:**

14 sets of 2 2x5mm orange coral discs

1 set of 3 2x5mm orange coral discs

5 8mm round turquoise beads

e. **31-inch (79 cm) strand – the finished strand with beads on it should measure 21 inches (53 cm) with plenty of excess wire for attaching the other end:**

6 sets of 2 2x5mm orange coral discs

1 set of 5 2 x 5mm orange coral discs

3 8mm round turquoise beads

3 15mm round flat turquoise beads

1 coral flower pendant on jump ring

5 Using the flat crimp technique, attach one strand of beading wire to each of the loops of the second end bar, ensuring that the shorter strand is at the top and working down to the longest strand at the bottom.

6. Use a jump ring to attach the lobster clasp one of the end bars.

7. Attach a jump ring to the second end bar to create the other half of the closure.

CHAPTER 4
Knotted Jewelry

Cord and Knotting

Working with cord (cotton, nylon, leather and more) is lots of fun because it allows you to create some fabulous effects by mixing beads and knots. You'll be amazed at the stunning designs you can create by using just a few simple knotting techniques.

Lark's head knot

This knot is often used to attach pendants such as donuts and medallions that cannot be simply strung on the cord. Fold length of cord in half.

1   Thread the fold of the cord through the hole of the donut or medallion.
2   Open the folded cord to form a loop and pass the cut ends of cord through the loop.
3   Pull tight.

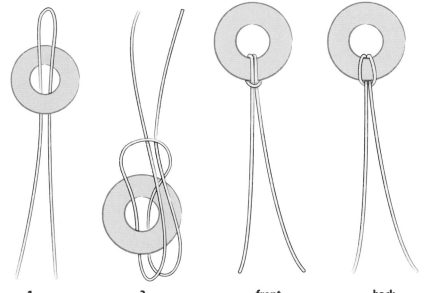

1   **2**   **front**   **back**

Overhand knot

1   Make a loop with the cord.
2   Bring the left side over the right side, and pass through the loop.
3   Pull to tighten.

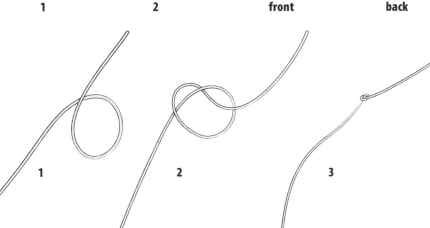

1   **2**   **3**

The square knots

The square and half-square knots in these projects are macramé knots, requiring one or two stationery center cords, as illustrated in the diagrams.

Half square knot

1   Bring cord A down and across (left to right) on top of the center cord or cords, leaving a space.

2   Pass cord B down, over cord A.

3   Pass cord B to the left behind the center cord(s).

4   Pass cord B through the loop space formed in step 1.

5   Tighten the knot by pulling both A and B.

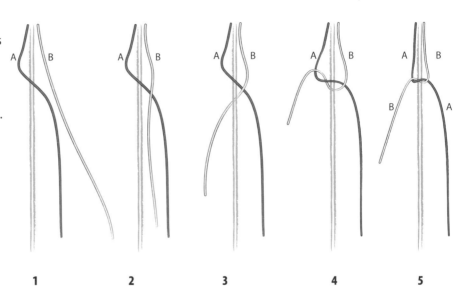

1   2   3   4   5

Square knot

1   Make a half square knot.

2   Reverse the process by starting again with cord A, which is now on the right. Bring cord A down and across (right to left) on top of the center cord(s).

3   Pass cord B down, over cord A.

4   Pass cord B behind the center cord(s).

5   Push cord B through the loop space formed in step 3.

6   Tighten the knot by pulling both A and B. (A and B are now back on their original sides of the work.)

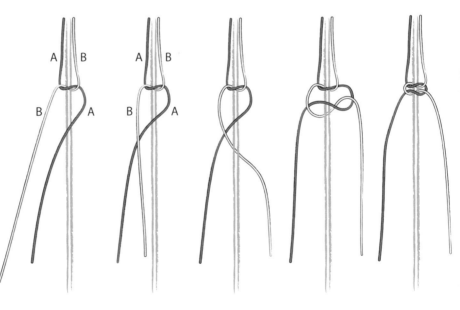

2   3   4   5   6

Loop and bead clasp

Making the loop side of the clasp

1. Fold cord, making a folded end and two strands of cord, side-by-side.

2. Close to the folded end, tie an overhand knot with this doubled cord. This is like any other overhand knot, except that the two strands are held together as one cord. The folded end becomes the loop of the closure.

3. Adjust loop size so it will fit over the bead you will be using at the other end. (The loop needs to be large enough to pass over the bead, but not so large that the bead can pass back through it too easily. You don't want the piece to slip off during wear.) Pull tight.

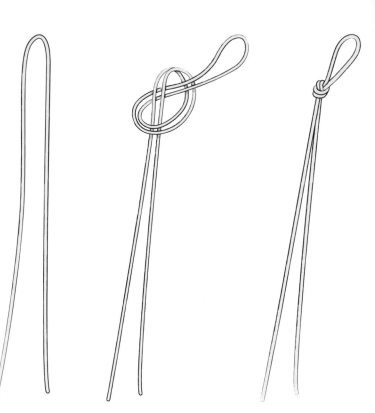

1   **2**   **3**

Making the bead side of the clasp

1 Tie an overhand knot just below where you want the bead to be positioned (allowing enough cord for tying an overhand knot on the other side of the bead).

2 Thread on the bead (if all strands won't fit through the hole, some can go around the outside of the bead, as shown).

3 Tie an overhand knot on the other end of the bead.

4 Tighten the knot so that the bead is held securely in place.

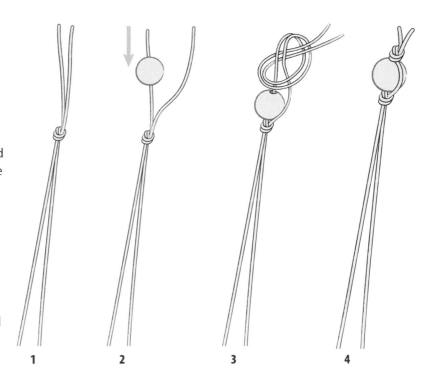

Attaching a cord coil

The size of the cord coil end finding should be close to the outside diameter of the cord or cords being used.

1 Apply adhesive such as G-S Hypo Cement to the inside of the cord coil finding.

2 Insert the neatly trimmed cord/cords into the coil.

3 Secure the cord by gently squeezing the last strand of the coil inwards using flat nose pliers.

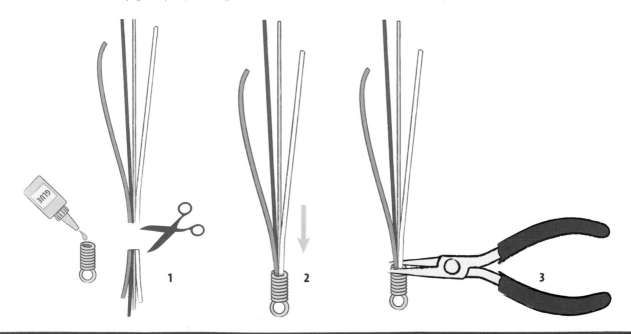

Black & Copper Necklace

The metalwork of these beads is styled after the silver beads of Bali and India. Substituting silver beads for the copper ones would suit this necklace just as well.

You will need...

approximately 197 inches (5 m) shiny black waxed cotton cord

31 assorted sizes of antiqued copper-colored large-holed metal beads

7 10x8mm AB black faceted beads

8 8x6mm AB black faceted beads

All you do is...

1 Cut the black cord into three strands of equal length. Hold all three strands together and fold in half. (Hint: tie the three cords together with a piece of yarn or contrasting thread at the fold to mark the center point of the necklace while you work.)

2 Holding all three strands together, tie an overhand knot ½ inch (1 cm) to the left of the center point.

3 Thread a copper bead onto one strand. Pull the outer strands around the bead and tie an overhand knot with all three strands. Pull the knot tight against the bead to hold it in place.

4 Measure 1 inch (2 cm) down, and tie another knot with all three strands.

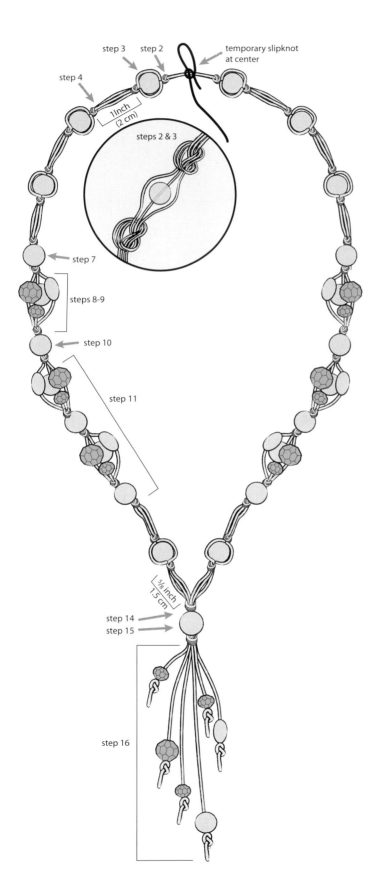

5 Repeat step 3-4.

6 Repeat step 3 once more.

7 Measure approximately 1 inch (2 cm) and, using all three strands, tie an overhand knot. Thread a copper bead onto all three strands of cord. Holding all three strands, tie another overhand knot.

8 Split the three strands of cord, and thread the following:

9 Strand 1: one copper bead and one small black faceted bead

10 Strand 2: one copper bead

11 Strand 3: one large black faceted bead

12 Using all three strands together, tie an overhand knot.

13 Thread a copper bead onto all three strands of cord. Using all three strands, tie another overhand knot.

14 Repeat steps 8 to 10.

15 Measure down 1 inch (2 cm), and tie another overhand knot with all three strands. Repeat step 3.

16 Repeat steps 3-12 on the other side of the necklace.

17 On both sides, measure approximately 5/8 inch (1.5 cm) from the last bead. Using all 6 strands, tie an overhand knot.

18 Thread all six strands through one large copper bead and use all six strands to tie an overhand knot.

19 Thread assorted beads onto each of the six strands. Place the beads at various and random lengths, each held in place with an overhand knot. Trim any excess cord.

Red & Black Cube & Tube Necklace

This is a variation of the red and black lacquer look, but with a cooler-toned red as an alternative to the more orange-red hues of the cinnabar. The knots in this necklace make attractive spacers.

You will need...

approximately 80 inches (2 m) black waxed cotton cord

9 20mm red marble faceted cube acrylic beads

16 10x32mm decorative resin tube beads

2 silver-plated cord coils

2 5mm silver-plated jump rings

1 silver-plated toggle clasp

All you do is...

1   Cut cord in half.

2   Attach both halves to a cord coil.

3   Tie the strands together in an overhand knot approximately 1¾ inches (4.5 cm) from the cord coil.

4   Split the cords apart and thread a resin tube onto each strand.

5   Tie the cords together in an overhand knot.

6   Thread both strands through a faceted cube bead.

7   Repeat step 5.

8   Repeat steps 4 through 7 three times.

9   Repeat steps 6 and 7 two times.

10 Repeat steps 4-7 three times

11 Repeat steps 4 and 5.

12 Cut cords about 2 inches (5 cm) from the last knot.

13 Attach both cords to a cord coil.

14 Attach the two parts of the toggle clasp to cord coils at either end of the necklace.

Patina Donut Necklace

The pendant in this necklace is reminiscent of the Chinese and Japanese coins and amulets that were, and are, often combined with special stones to draw properties such as luck, serenity and friendship to the wearer.

You will need...

about 6½ feet (2 m) tan waxed cotton cord

about 6½ feet (2 m) brown waxed cotton cord

patina copper metal donut

20 10mm round faceted glass beads – tan/aqua mix

2 small round copper colored coil leather crimps

1 5mm copper colored jump rings

22mm lobster clasp

9mm copper colored jump ring

All you do is...

1 Cut the tan and brown cords in half.

2 Bundle the four halves into a single cord and, using a lark's head knot, attach the patina donut.

3 Split the cords into the two sides of the necklace (two of each color on each side).

4 Thread an assortment of the glass beads at random positions over 3¾ inches (9.5 cm), tying an overhand knot on either side of each bead to hold it in place.

5 Holding all four cords together, tie an overhand knot.

6 Repeat steps 4 and 5.

7 Measure 4 inches (10 cm) and cut off excess cord.

8 Attach a cord coil to the four strands.

9 Repeat on the other side of the necklace.

10 Use a 5mm jump ring to attach the lobster clasp to one cord coil.

11 Attach a 9mm jump ring to the other cord coil.

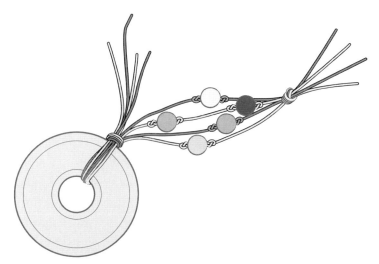

Black Knot Choker

Ornamental knotting is an ancient craft that never goes out of style. Knots have decorated garments, furniture and, of course, jewelry. Different knot designs symbolize blessings such as joy and prosperity. The Chinese button knot featured here is a symbol of good luck.

You will need...

about 13 feet (4 m) black waxed cotton cord

4 25x15mm cord covered tube beads – black & tan

1 18x22mm cord covered round bead – black & tan

7 15x18mm black cord knot beads

All you do is...

1   Cut the black cord in half and, holding the two strands together, fold in half.

2   Tie an overhand knot about 1 inch (2.5 cm) from the fold, forming a loop.

3   Using the two inner strands as your center cord, tie half square knots (see page 49) for about ¾ inch (2 cm) This will spiral around.

4   Thread a cord knot bead onto all four strands.

5   Repeat step 3.

6   Thread a tube bead onto all four strands of cord.

7   Repeat step 3.

8   Thread the following beads onto all four strands of cord:

black cord knot bead

tube bead

black cord knot bead

round bead

black cord knot bead

tube bead

black cord knot bead

9   Repeat steps 3 and 6.

10 Repeat step 3 and 4 two times.

11 Tie an overhand knot above the last knot bead, using all four strands.

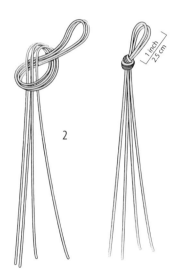

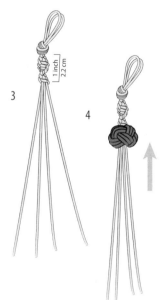

Amethyst Shamballa Bracelet

You will need...

approximately 60 inches
(1.5 m) 1.2mm thick black
woven nylon cord

a separate length of
approximately 20 inches
(.5 m) 1.2mm thick cord

approximately 20 inches
(.5 m) .8mm thick black
woven nylon cord

6 10mm amethyst beads

2 6mm amethyst beads

3 10mm amethyst color
pave' beads

The Shamballa Bracelet (also Shambala or Shambhala) takes its name from the Buddhist tradition's mythical place of spiritual enlightenment. Part fashion trend, part spiritual expression, this bracelet is thought to support peace in the mind and heart of the wearer.

Shamballa bracelets are made from all kinds of property-bearing stones and metals. In some bracelets each bead is made of a different substance. Many if not most include one or more glittery pave' beads for sparkle and energy. Some may consist entirely of pave' beads, and others have none at all. Infinite variety is part of the fun and beauty of the Shamballa bracelet.

All you do is...

1   Use clear nail polish and coat approximately ¾ inch (2 cm) of the cut ends of the thinner cord (called the **core cord**). Use your fingers to work the polish into the cord and allow to dry. This will stiffen the end, making it easier to pass through the holes of the beads. When dry, cut the tips at an angle – again, to help when threading through beads.

2   Fold the long (60-inch/1.5 m), thicker cord in half to find the middle. Lay the core cord over the center fold (with approximately 4 inches [10 cm] extending above).

3   Use the strands of thicker cord to make a square knot around the core cord. See diagrams 1-10 (above right) and/or the diagrams for the square knot on page 49. Pull this and all knots tight for a more pleasing and symmetrical finish. Tip: It is helpful to secure the core cord to a clipboard or attach the top end to a smooth surface with tape.

4   Make 3 more square knots for a total of 4. Tip: These instructions make a bracelet, approximately 7-7½ inches (18-19 cm) long. For a larger bracelet, you can add one or more square knots here.

5   String a 10mm amethyst bead onto the core cord up to the last knot from step 4. Bring the thick cord around the bead and tie a square knot below the bead.

6   Repeat step 5 with the remaining 10mm beads, placed in the following order: 2 more 10mm amethyst beads, the 3 10mm pave' beads, and finishing with the 3 remaining 10mm amethyst beads.

7   Tie a total of four square knots after the last bead placed in step 6.

8   Cut the excess thick cords about 1/8 inch (3 mm) from the last knot and use the heat from a flame (or invest in a battery-powered Thread Zapper) to melt the ends of the nylon cord. The nylon cord will shrink back as it melts and attach to the nylon cord around it, creating a neatly sealed knot.

9   Now is a good time to measure the length of your bracelet to determine how long the slide closure should be. The length so far will be determined by

1   2   3

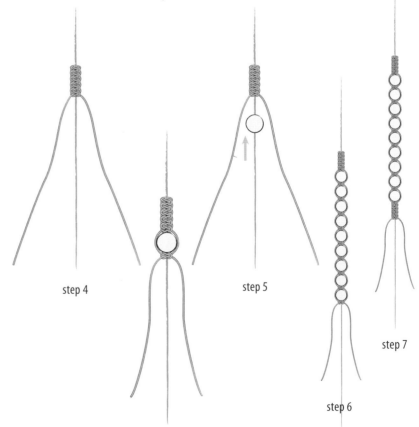

step 4   step 5   step 7

step 6

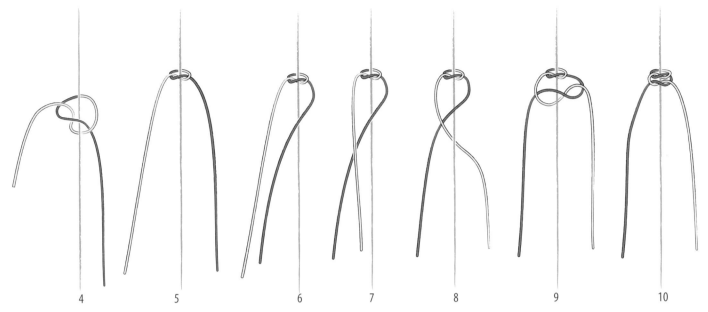

4   5   6   7   8   9   10

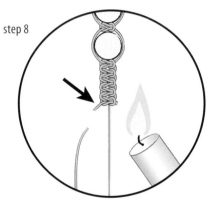

step 8

how tight or loose you tie your knots. Measure from the beginning of the knots in step 3 to the last knot in step 7. Try the bracelet on for size. Subtract the length of your bracelet so far from the length you wish it to be when it is completed. This is the length you will need for your slide closure.

10 Pull the core cord until the two ends are of equal length. Bring the two ends around past each other to form a loop (so it looks like a bracelet with cord ends running alongside each other in different directions (see diagram).

11 To make a slide closure, take the shorter (20-inch/.5 m) 1.2mm cord and tie a series of square knots around the two core cords (see diagram). When you have enough square knots to equal the length of your slide closure (as per step 9), try on the bracelet to make sure it fits. This is your last opportunity to eliminate knots to shorten or add knots to lengthen the bracelet.

12 Repeat step 8 with the excess thick cords to seal.

13 String a 6mm semi precious amethyst bead onto each end of the core cord. Tie an overhand knot at the end, in the position where you want the bead to hang. Be sure to leave enough of the core cord to pull the bracelet open to slip over your hand. By pulling on these smaller beads, you will be able to close the bracelet to fit your wrist.

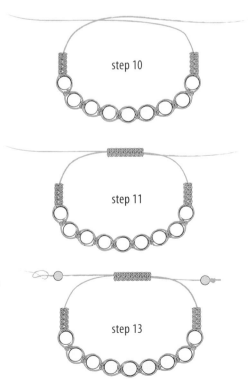

step 10

step 11

step 13

Pink Flower Green Macramé Choker

The pink and green of this macramé piece recalls the look of cherry blossoms in spring. This is an interesting combination of bright and soft, as well as a contrast of textures.

You will need...

approximately 158 inches (4 m) green waxed cotton cord

8 12mm round white porcelain/pink flower beads

10 4x6mm antiqued pewter spacer beads

6 15mm antiqued pewter bead caps

All you do is...

1   Cut the cord into three equal lengths. Hold all three strands together.

2   At one end, make the "loop side" of a loop and bead clasp (see page 50) . This loop should fit snugly but comfortably around a pink flower porcelain bead.

3   With two of the strands of cord, repeatedly tie a half square knot (see page 49) around the third (center) strand for 4 inches (8 cm). This will spiral around.

4   Thread a pewter spacer bead onto the center strand of cord. (All beads will be strung on this core strand.) Bring the outer strands around the bead and tie a square knot below the bead.

5   Thread on a porcelain bead. Bring the outer strands around the bead and tie a square knot.

6   Thread on a pewter spacer bead. Bring the outer strands around the bead and tie 3 square knots.

7   Thread on a bead cap, a porcelain bead, and another bead cap. Bring the outer strands around the bead and tie 3 square knots.

8   Thread on a pewter spacer bead. Bring the outer strands around the bead and tie a square knot.

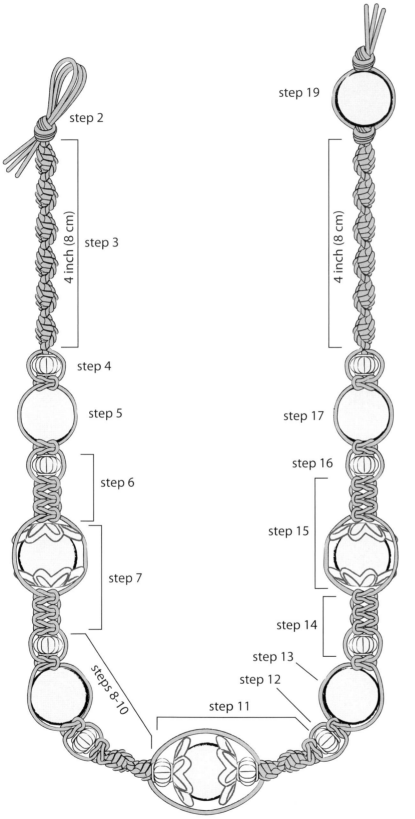

step 2

step 3

4 inch (8 cm)

step 4

step 5

step 6

step 7

steps 8-10

step 11

step 12

step 13

step 14

step 15

step 16

step 17

step 19

4 inch (8 cm)

9 Thread on a porcelain bead. Bring the outer strands around the bead and tie a square knot.

10 Thread on a pewter spacer bead. Bring the outer strands around the bead and tie a square knot, then tie half square knots (spiraling around) for about ½ inch (1 cm).

11 Thread on a pewter spacer bead, a bead cap, a porcelain bead (this is the center bead of the choker), a bead cap and a pewter spacer bead. Bring the outer strands around all the beads and tie half square knots for about ½ inch (1 cm). Tie a square knot.

12 Thread on a pewter spacer bead. Bring the outer strands around the bead and tie 3 square knots.

13 Thread on a porcelain bead. Bring the outer strands around the bead and tie a square knot.

14 Thread on a pewter spacer bead. Bring the outer strands around the bead and tie 3 square knots.

15 Thread on a bead cap, a porcelain bead and a bead cap. Bring the outer strands around the bead and tie 3 square knots.

16 Thread on a pewter spacer bead. Bring the outer strands around the bead and tie a square knot.

17 Thread on a porcelain bead. Bring the outer strands around the bead and tie a square knot.

18 Thread on a pewter spacer bead. Bring the outer strands around the bead and repeatedly tie a half square knot for 4 inches (8 cm).

19 Bundle the three strands together to tie an overhand knot. On the center strand thread a porcelain bead. Bring the outer strands around the bead and bundle the three strands to tie another overhand knot. Trim any excess cord, but not too close.

CHAPTER 5

Loop And Chain Jewelry

Making Loops and Working with Chain

Making loops with wire is one of the essential basics for jewelry making. Although it takes a little practice, being able to make loops will open a multitude of new options for designing and creating your own unique jewelry.

Basic technique for making single loops

In the same way that you made dangles for memory wire bracelets, thread bead(s) onto an eye or head pin.

1 Bend the wire extending above bead(s) at a right angle, as close to bead as possible.

2 Cut off excess wire, leaving a small arm of 3/8 inch (1 cm)

3 Using the tip of the round nose pliers, grab the cut end and curl wire back towards body of pin, wrapping it around one round barrel of the pliers. The loop should then be positioned centrally over the hole of the bead.

Opening and closing loops

1 To open the loop, grasp the loop with either a single pair or two pairs of flat nose pliers.

2 Twist the open end to the side, just enough to allow the jump ring, chain link, etc. to slip through, as in diagram 2, right.

3 Do not pull the loop open as shown in diagram 3, right. It weakens the wire and makes it hard to properly close the loop again.

4 To close the loop, twist back in place.

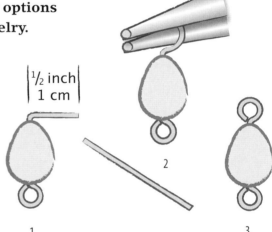

½ inch
1 cm

1

2

3

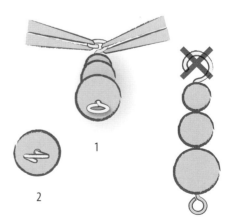

1

2

3

Opening and closing a jump ring (or a link of chain)

1   Grasp each side of the join, using two pairs of flat nose (or chain nose or bent nose) pliers.

2   To open, carefully twist jump ring ends apart. Do not pull apart!

3   To close, twist jump ring ends back together, going slightly past each other then bring back (they usually click into place and you can feel them rub together) for a perfect fit.

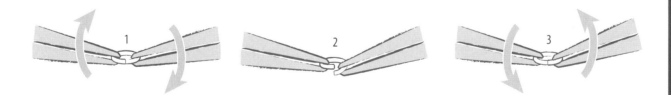

Making a bracelet, necklace or earrings with chain

1   Cut chain to the desired length.

2   This can be done by twisting open one link of chain, and unhooking it from the rest of the chain. (Most chain links have a split at one end, somewhat like a jump ring.)

3   Or, you can cut a link using a wire cutter. Do take care, and wear eye protection when cutting wires or chains.

Abalone Shell Ensemble

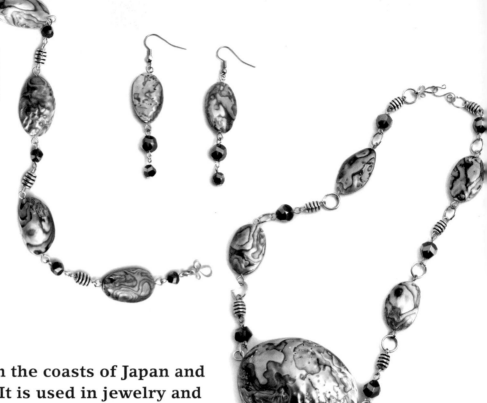

Abalone can be found on the coasts of Japan and on other Pacific shores. It is used in jewelry and inlaid artwork from all parts of Asia and is particularly beautiful when paired with silver.

Necklace
You will need...

1 55mm closed abalone shell

4 approx. 25x16mm closed abalone shells

6 8mm round faceted AB purple beads

6 5x7mm antiqued silver-plated metal tube beads

16 ½-inch (38mm) silver-plated eye pins

1 3-inch (75mm) silver-plated eye pin

12 7mm silver-plated jump rings

12mm silver-plated fancy hook & eye clasp

All you do is...

1 Thread the large abalone shell onto the long eye pin and form a loop at the other end.

2 Make 6 bead units (A) with a purple faceted bead.

3 Make 6 bead units (B) with a silver tube bead.

4 Make 4 bead units (C) with a small abalone shell.

5 Use a 7mm jump ring to join an A unit to one side of the large abalone shell.

6 Join a B unit to the A unit from step 5.

7 Use a 7mm jump ring to join a C unit to the B unit from step 6.

8 Use a 7mm jump ring to join an A unit to the other side the C unit from step 7.

9 Repeat steps 6-8.

10 Join a B unit to the A unit from step 8.

11 Use a 7mm jump ring to join one half of the clasp to the B unit from step 10.

12 Repeat steps 5 –11 on the other side of the large abalone shell.

Bracelet
You will need...

4 approx. 25x16mm closed abalone shells

4 6mm round faceted AB purple beads

4 5x7mm antiqued silver-plated metal tube beads

12 ½-inch (38mm) silver-plated eye pins

2 5mm silver-plated jump rings

1 12 mm silver-plated fancy hook & eye clasp

Earrings
What you need is...

2 approx. 25x16mm closed abalone shells

2 8mm round faceted AB purple beads

2 6mm round faceted AB purple beads

4 1½ inch (38mm) silver-plated eye pins

2 1½ inch (38mm) silver-plated head pins

2 silver-plated ear wires

All you do is...

1 Make 4 bead units (A) with a purple faceted bead.

2 Make 4 bead units (B) with a small abalone shell.

3 Make 4 bead units (C) with a silver tube bead.

4 Join one each of units A and C to either end of a unit B.

5 Repeat 3 more times.

6 Use the 5mm jump rings to attach the hook and eye clasp parts to either end of the chain of beads.

All you do is...

1 Using an eye pin, make a bead unit (A) with a small abalone shell.

2 Using an eye pin, make a bead unit (B) with an 8mm purple faceted bead.

3 Using a head pin, make a bead unit (C) with a 6mm purple faceted bead.

4 Join units A and C to either end of unit B.

5 Attach the other end of the A unit to an ear wire.

6 Repeat steps 1 to 5 for the second earring.

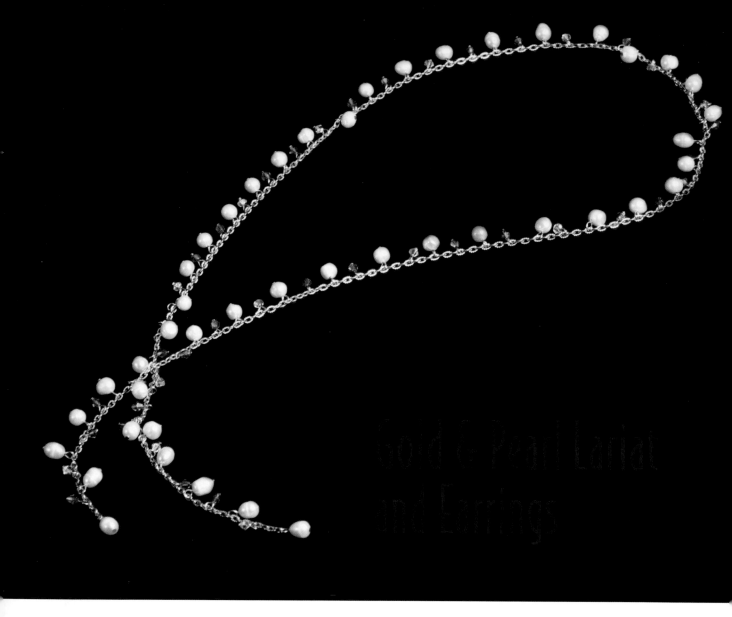

Gold & Pearl Lariat and Earrings

Necklace – You will need...

about 39½ inches (1 m) fancy fine gold-plated chain (with approx. 7 links per ½ inch [1 cm])

46 (approx.) oval freshwater pearls

30 4mm AB amber faceted bicone beads

16 4mm AB clear faceted bicone beads

92 (approx.) 1½ inch (38mm) gold-plated head pins

The many shapes and tints of natural pearls make these gems a versatile component in any style of jewelry. The oval shape of these pearls works wonderfully in this long necklace, inspired by a border pattern in a Persian rug.

NOTE: Genuine pearls are very finely drilled. When using freshwater pearls, use fine gauge head pins (about 24 or 26 gauge).

All you do is...

1. Make each pearl and bicone into a simple dangle.

2. Fold the chain so that one end is about 1½ inches (4 cm) longer than the other.

3. Open the loop of one pearl unit and use it to join the two strands of chain at about 6 inches (15 cm) from the longer end, leaving two uneven tails.

4. From the pearl placed in step 3, count up 4 links of chain and hang an amber bicone on the outside of the chain link. Repeat on opposite side of necklace.

5. Count up 4 links of chain and hang a pearl unit on the outside of the chain link. Repeat on opposite side of necklace.

6. Count up 4 links of chain and hang an amber bicone unit on the outside of the chain link. Repeat on opposite side of necklace.

7. Count up 4 links of chain and hang a pearl unit on the outside of the chain link. Repeat on opposite side of necklace.

8. Count up 4 links of chain and hang a clear bicone unit on the outside of the chain link. Repeat on opposite side of necklace.

9. Count up 4 links of chain and hang a pearl unit on the outside of the chain link. Repeat on opposite side of necklace.

10. Count up 4 links of chain and hang an amber bicone unit on the outside of the chain link. Repeat on opposite side of necklace.

11. Repeat the pattern of amber bicone, pearl, clear bicone, pearl, amber bicone – each bead 4 chain links apart – until the chain above and below where the chain is joined (step 3) is filled with beads dangling on the outside of the chain.

12. Hang a pearl unit from each end.

Earrings – You will need...

about 10¾ inches (27 cm) fancy fine gold-plated chain (approx. 7 links per ½ inch/1 cm)

14 (approx.) oval freshwater pearls

8 4mm AB amber faceted bicones

4 4mm AB clear faceted bicones

26 (approx.) 1½ inch (38mm) gold-plated head pins

2 gold-plated ear wires

All you do is...

1 Cut a piece of chain approximately 2½ inches (6 cm) long and a second piece of chain 3 inches (7.5 cm) long.

2 Attach both pieces of chain to the loop of an ear wire.

3 As per the lariat, make each pearl and bicone into a simple dangle.

4 On the longer chain, attach a pearl to the bottom end.

5 Count 4 links up from the pearl and attach a clear bicone bead.

6 Continue to count 4 links up from the previous bead and add: a second pearl, an amber bicone, a third pearl, a second amber bicone and a fourth pearl.

7 On the shorter piece of chain attach a pearl to the bottom end.

8 Count 4 links up from the pearl and add an amber bicone.

9 Continue to count 4 links up from the previous bead and add: a second pearl, a clear bicone, a third pearl and a second amber bicone bead.

10 Repeat steps 1-8 to make the second earring.

Red & Black Resin Bead Necklace

The smaller round beads in this necklace add Chinese characters to the red and black color combination.

You will need...

7 22x20mm engraved resin beads

7 14x16mm engraved resin beads

28 10mm matte black onyx rondelle beads

14 4x14mm red coral rondelle beads

14 7x7mm antiqued gold-plated pewter beads

42 3mm round gold-plated beads

28 gold-plated eye pins, assorted lengths

All you do is...

1 Make 7 bead units (A) on an eye pin. These and all the bead units are finished by forming a loop at the top of the last bead.

1 antiqued gold-plated pewter bead

1 22x20mm engraved resin bead

1 antiqued gold-plated pewter bead

2 Make 14 bead units (B).

1 round gold bead

1 black onyx rondelle

1 red coral rondelle

1 round gold bead

3 Make 7 bead units (C).

1 round gold bead

1 14x16mm engraved resin bead

1 round gold bead

4 Join the three different bead units together in the following order:

unit A

unit B

unit C

unit B

5 Repeat 6 more times and join to the other end to complete this lovely, long necklace that slips over the head—no clasp needed!

Etched Resin Choker

Curls and swirls have been used to represent many things in Asian art— waves, clouds, the mane of a lion, the branches on a tree, and more. The curls, coin motif and ivory tones combine to give this choker a fun Asian flavor.

All you do is...

1 Cut two lengths of chain with 59 links each. You should have about 4 inches (8 cm) left over.

2 Pass a head pin through one black bicone bead, then through the 6th link of one chain. Continue by passing the head pin through a black oval bead, then the 6th link of the other chain strand. Pass the head pin through a second black bicone, and form a loop.

3 Pass a head pin through a black bicone bead and a heart bead and form a loop. Attach to the head pin loop formed in step 2.

4 Pass a head pin through one black bicone bead, then through the 4th loop from the bead unit with the oval black bead. Continue by passing through a diamond-shaped bead, then through the 4th link of the other chain strand. Finish by passing the head pin through a second black bicone and forming a loop.

5 Pass a head pin through a round black bead and form a loop. Attach to the loop formed in step 4.

6 Continue to place bead units with a black oval bead with a heart dangle (as in steps 2 and 3) and bead units with a diamond bead (as in step 4) alternating them, with 3 links between each unit, until there are a total of 7 black oval bead units and 6 diamond shaped bead units.

7 Pass a head pin through a round black bead and form a loop. Make 25 of these units. Attach one unit to the central link between each of the black oval beads and diamond shaped beads on both strands of chain.

8 Attach the last unit to the end of the short piece of remaining chain (about 8 links). Set aside. This will be the extension chain.

9 Join the two strands of chain together with a jump ring on either end. On one end, add the lobster clasp before closing the jump ring.

10 Attach the extension chain to the other end of the choker using another jump ring.

2

3

4

5
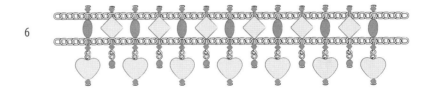

6

7

8

9 & 10

Flower & Butterfly Charm Bracelet

**The blossoms, butterflies, and soft pink beads
in this bracelet are like fabric for a spring
kimono. A floral clasp adds an extra nice touch.**

You will need...

about 7 inches (17 cm) shiny silver curb chain (approx. 27 links in total)

8 10mm peach colored glass flower beads

4 6mm antiqued pewter flower beads

5 assorted antiqued pewter butterfly beads

5 8x6mm pale peach faceted crystal beads

9 small white freshwater pearl beads

9 small antique rose freshwater pearls

8 11/0 silver metallic seed beads

13 2-inch (50mm) small ball (1.2mm) silver-plated head pins

27 1½ inch (38 mm) silver-plated head pins

1 antiqued pewter flower hook and eye clasp

All you do is...

1 Open the link on either end of the chain. Attach the hook half of the clasp to one end of the chain and the loop half to the other. Close links.

2 On a ball-end head pin thread a glass flower bead and a silver seed bead and form a loop. Repeat with the remaining flower beads.

3 On a ball-end head pin thread the faceted peach crystal beads and form a loop. Repeat with the remaining crystal beads.

4 On a plain head pin thread a pewter flower bead and form a loop. Repeat with the remaining pewter flower beads.

5 On a plain head pin string a butterfly bead and form a loop. Repeat with the remaining butterfly beads.

6 On a plain head pin thread a freshwater pearl and form a loop. Repeat with the remaining freshwater pearls (both white and rose).

7 Attach all the beads to the chain bracelet as follows:

Links 1, 5, 7, 11, 15, 17, 21, 23, 27 - 1 white and 1 rose freshwater pearl

Links 2, 10, 18, 26 - 1 pewter flower bead

Links 3, 9, 13, 19, 25 - 1 faceted peach crystal bead

Links 4, 8, 14, 20, 24 - 1 pewter butterfly bead

Links 6, 12, 16, 22 - 2 peach glass flower beads

Elephant & Jade Bracelet

In Asia, the elephant symbolizes many things, among them wisdom, dignity and peace. Here, silver elephants are enhanced by the beauty and virtue of jade.

Necklace
You will need...

about 7 inches (17 cm) large silver-plated curb chain (10x15mm)

about 8 inches (20 cm) medium silver-plated curb chain (6x8mm)

about 8 inches (20 cm) medium rhodium-plated curb chain (4x6mm)

3 large silver-plated charms (30x35mm elephant)

2 small silver-plated charms (12x20mm elephant)

approximately 150 small jade chips

6 9mm silver-plated jump rings

2 7mm silver-plated jump rings

150 1½ inch (38mm) silver-plated head pins

1 large silver-plated clasp hook

All you do is...

1   Open the link that is one in from the end of the large chain. Thread one end of each of the other two chains onto the large chain and then close the link.

2   Weave one medium chain in and out through the links of the large chain, and attach to the last link of the large chain with a 9mm jump ring.

3   Starting your weave from the opposite side/direction, weave the second medium chain through the links. Attach to the last chain using the same jump ring as step 2.

4   Use 9mm jump rings to attach the elephant charms to the woven chain bracelet, equal distance apart.

5   Make bead units from the jade chips by threading them onto a head pin and forming a loop. Attach the jade units to the two medium chains. Work from both sides of the main chain and space the units as evenly as you can.

6   Use two 7mm jump rings to attach the silver clasp hook to the jump ring from steps 2 and 3.

Earrings
You will need...

6 small jade chips

2 links from medium silver curb chain, separated

6 silver-plated head pins

2 silver-plated ear wires

2 7mm jump rings

All you do is...

1   Make jade bead units by threading each chip onto a head pin and forming a loop.

2   On each jump ring attach one unit.

3   On one link hang a bead unit, a unit with jump ring, and another unit. Attach an ear wire before closing link. Repeat for second earring.

Over 25 years of jewelry-making experience have left me with the strong belief that with a few basic techniques, some beautiful beads and good components, anyone can create a lovely piece of jewelry. Your own imagination and sense of style are key to making any piece—even one based on a project in a book, magazine or website—a unique creation. My hope is that this book has provided not only some basic techniques, but also some inspiring ideas that will help you make every piece you create an individual work of art.

Resources

Jewelry-making tools and materials are easy to find. In addition to suppliers listed here, check your local area for bead shops (they thrive on your support) and look at listings and ads in the many fantastic beading magazines that are available.

USA

The selection of tools, beads and findings in local craft stores just gets better and better. Some offer quality metal findings as well as economy ones, and beads ranging from plastic to semi–precious. Check out:

Jo-Ann Fabrics & Crafts

Hobby Lobby

AC Moore

Michael's

Some of the following online resources also have street stores and showrooms, so if you're local or will be visiting the area, check the websites for store locations and hours.

USA

Fire Mountain Gems & Beads – www.firemountaingems.com (Grants Pass, OR)

Artbeads – www.artbeads.com (Gig Harbor, WA)

Fusion Beads – www.fusionbeads.com (Seattle, WA)

Shipwreck Beads – www.shipwreckbeads.com (Lacey, WA)

Beadazzled – www.beadazzled.net (Washington, DC; Baltimore, MD; McLean, VA)

Pikake Beads – www.pikake–beads.com (Kailua–Kona, HI)

The Bead Lounge – www.thebeadlounge.net (Orlando, FL)

Lima Beads – www.limabeads.com (Ann Arbor, MI)

Rio Grande – www.riogrande.com (Albuquerque, NM)

JewelrySupply – www.jewelrysupply.com (Roseville, CA)

The Bead Goes On – www.thebeadgoeson.com (Virginia Beach, VA)

Happy Mango Beads – www.happymangobeads.com (Berthoud, CO)

UK

Beads Unlimited – www.beadsunlimited.co.uk

Bijoux by Me – www.bijouxbyme.co.uk

Beaders Companion – www.beaderscompanion.co.uk

Creative Beadcraft – www.creativebeadcraft.co.uk

Special thanks to the following suppliers for contributing materials for these projects:

Chris and Steve at Solid Oak (distributor of beads and components)

Steve and Wyatt at Beadalon (manufacturer/distributor of components)

Dino and Gary at Bijoux by Me (online retailer of beads and components)

Fire Mountain Gems & Beads (online retailer of beads and components)

Index

Published by Tuttle Publishing, an imprint of Periplus Editions (HK) Ltd.

www.tuttlepublishing.com

Library of Congress Cataloging-in-Publication Data

Schulz, Carolyn.
  Creative beaded jewelry : 33 exquisite designs inspired by the arts of China, Japan, India and Tibet / by Carolyn Schulz.
    pages cm
    Includes index.
  ISBN 978-0-8048-4301-0 (pbk.)
1. Bead work. 2. Jewelry. I. Title.
  TT860.S38 2012
  745.594'2--dc23
                            2012028876

ISBN 978-0-8048-4301-0

Distributed by

North America, Latin America & Europe
Tuttle Publishing
364 Innovation Drive
North Clarendon, VT 05759-9436 U.S.A.
Tel: 1 (802) 773-8930
Fax: 1 (802) 773-6993
info@tuttlepublishing.com
www.tuttlepublishing.com

Japan
Tuttle Publishing
Yaekari Building,
3rd Floor, 5-4-12 Osaki
Shinagawa-ku, Tokyo 141 0032
Tel: (81) 3 5437-0171
Fax: (81) 3 5437-0755
sales@tuttle.co.jp
www.periplus.com

Asia Pacific
Berkeley Books Pte. Ltd.
61 Tai Seng Avenue
#02-12, Singapore 534167
Tel: (65) 6280-1330
Fax: (65) 6280-6290
inquiries@periplus.com.sg
www.periplus.com

First edition
17 16 15 14 13   6 5 4 3 2 1

Printed in Singapore   1301TW

The Tuttle Story: "Books to Span the East and West"

Most people are surprised to learn that the world's largest publisher of books on Asia had its humble beginnings in the tiny American state of Vermont. The company's founder, Charles Tuttle, came from a New England family steeped in publishing, and his first love was books—especially old and rare editions.

Tuttle's father was a noted antiquarian dealer in Rutland, Vermont. Young Charles honed his knowledge of the trade working in the family bookstore, and later in the rare books section of Columbia University Library. His passion for beautiful books—old and new—never wavered throughout his long career as a bookseller and publisher.

After graduating from Harvard, Tuttle enlisted in the military and in 1945 was sent to Tokyo to work on General Douglas MacArthur's staff. He was tasked with helping to revive the Japanese publishing industry, which had been utterly devastated by the war. When his tour of duty was completed, he left the military, married a talented and beautiful singer, Reiko Chiba, and in 1948 began several successful business ventures.

To his astonishment, Tuttle discovered that postwar Tokyo was actually a book-lover's paradise. He befriended dealers in the Kanda district and began supplying rare Japanese editions to American libraries. He also imported American books to sell to the thousands of GIs stationed in Japan. By 1949, Tuttle's business was thriving, and he opened Tokyo's very first English-language bookstore in the Takashimaya Department Store in Ginza, to great success. Two years later, he began publishing books to fulfill the growing interest of foreigners in all things Asian.

Though a westerner, Tuttle was hugely instrumental in bringing a knowledge of Japan and Asia to a world hungry for information about the East. By the time of his death in 1993, he had published over 6,000 books on Asian culture, history and art—a legacy honored by Emperor Hirohito in 1983 with the "Order of the Sacred Treasure," the highest honor Japan bestows upon non-Japanese.

The Tuttle company today maintains an active backlist of some 1,500 titles, many of which have been continuously in print since the 1950s and 1960s—a great testament to Charles Tuttle's skill as a publisher. More than 60 years after its founding, Tuttle Publishing is more active today than at any time in its history, still inspired by Charles Tuttle's core mission—to publish fine books to span the East and West and provide a greater understanding of each.